MW00509234

Spiritual Autobiography

and

Meditation Handbook

By

Emerson Dean Brooking, Ph.D.

©2014 Emerson Dean Brooking, Ph.D.

Emerson Dean Brooking, Ph.D.

Panther Brook Spiritual Center

P.O. Box 55

1000 Panther Brook Lane

Turnerville, Georgia 30580

emerson@pantherbrook.com

www.pantherbrook.com

ISBN-13:   978-0615961750 (Panther Brook Spiritual Center)

ISBN-10: 0615961754

Publisher: Panther Brook Spiritual Center

Publication Date: January 24, 2014

Contents

Introduction – 1

Childhood – 2
Reverend Cato Dick – 2
Practice for the Ministry – 2

Adolescence – 3
Molestation – 4
Education as Key to Peace and Happiness – 4

Introduction to Meditation – 5
Meeting the Monk – 5
Return Visits to Wat Srigeat – 7
Meeting the Abbot – 9
My Studies at the Wat – 10
Graduation and a Buddha Image – 13

Bangkok, Thailand – 16

Koh Samui, Thailand – 18

Buddhist or Christian? – Penang, Malaysia – 21

A Monk's Letter – 23

Introduction to Serenity Meditation – 26

Serenity Meditation Instructions – 27

First Vipassana Meditation Retreat – 30
Meditation Not Just Being High – It is Solid! – 31

Mindfulness (Vipassana) Meditation Instructions – 32

Death of "Personal I" – A Dream – 34

Introduction to Progressive Muscle Relaxation – 36

Progressive Muscle Relaxation Instructions – 37

Southern Dharma Retreat Center – 40

Vipassana Meditation on the Mountain Top – 41

The Small Heavenly Microcosmic Orbit – 43

"Stream Entry" – A Dream and Interpretation – 46

Overwhelming Sorrow – 47

Join Cardiac Rehabilitation Team – 49

Meet my Guru – Roy Eugene Davis – 50

Initiation into Kriya Yoga and Kriya Pranayama
Meditation – 52

In the Eye of the Hurricane – Dad's Transition – 53

A New Year's Retreat – 55
The Inner Sound – 57

Himalayan Institute – 58
Thermal Biofeedback – 60
Electrodermal Biofeedback – 62
The Crocodile Posture – 64
Neti (Nasal) Wash – 65

Reverend Bo Turner – 66
Follower of Christ – 67
Bo's Transition – 67
God is Without Form and Name – 67

First Yoga Class – 68

Diaphragmatic Breathing Exercise – 69

Alternate Nostril Breathing – 71

Professional Biofeedback Training – 73

Introduction to Autogenic Training – 74

Autogenic Training Instructions – 75

Twenty-four Hour Retreats at Panther Brook
Spiritual Center – 77

1993 Thanksgiving Freedom from Addiction
Celebration – 77
Addictions are Spiritual Diseases – 79
1969 – Acid and Woodstock – 79
First Acid Trip – 80
Third Acid Trip – 81
A Week of Acid – 83
Acid Flashbacks – 83
Timothy Leary – 84
Consciousness Research – 84
Finding God-consciousness – 85
Physiological Explanation – 85
Spiritual Explanation – 86
Caffeine Addiction and the Inner Sound – 86

Technique of Primordial Sound and Light
Contemplation – 87

Behavioral Medicine Applications – 89

The Relaxation Response – 90
The *Fight-or-Flight* Response – 90
The Counterbalancing Relaxation Response – 92

Learning to Elicit the Relaxation Response – 92
Spirituality – 94

Relaxation Response Instructions – 95

Focus Word or Phrase – 96

Common Focus Words or Phrases –97

"Mini" Relaxation Exercises – 98
Ways to "do a mini" – 98
Mini versions 1, 2, & 3 – 99
Good times to "do a mini"... – 99

Restitution – Working the Steps – 100

Integral Yoga® Teacher Training – 101
Union with God – 102
God is Peace and Happiness Within – 104
I Passed!!! – 104

Yoga Philosophy – 105

Integral Yoga® – 107

Raja Yoga: The Yoga of Meditation – 108

Koshas – 109

The Breath of Life – 111

Prana: The Vital Force – 111
Pranayama: Controlling the Cosmic Power – 112
Yogic Breathing – 112
Benefits of Pranayama – 113

Sivananda Ashram Yoga Retreat – 115
Amrita and Fasting – 115
Pink Tongue – 118
Women – 119

My First Christian Centering Prayer Retreat – 121
Not Teaching Religion but God-realization – 121
False Self and True Self – 122

The Method of Christian Centering Prayer – 123
The Guidelines – 123
Contemplative Prayer – 123
The Method – 124
Explanation of the Guidelines – 124
Some Practical Points – 126
Points for Further Development – 127

Catastrophic Loss – 128
Pratipaksha Bhavana – 129

Intermediate Hatha Yoga Teacher Training – 131
God Enters my Heart – 131
Reproachfulness – 132
I Failed!!! – 133

Consultation with Dr. Jack Woodard – 134

Stress Management Teacher Training – 136
I Passed!!! – 136
Stress Cycle – 137

Yoga and Toccoa, Georgia – 137

September 11, 2001 – 141

Meher Baba's Spiritual Center – 142
The Seven Realities – 143

Being Lived by the Tao – 144

"Kundalini Crisis" – 145

A Note from my Abbot and Teacher – 150

Meher Spiritual Center – My Second Spiritual Hospital – 151
Emptiness – Meditation in Baba's Bedroom – 152
Spiritual Advancement – 153

Legacy – 155

Teacher Training at Center for Spiritual Awareness – 155

Living my Dream – 156

Driving While God Intoxicated – 157

Roy Eugene Davis Authorizes Teaching Kriya Yoga – 158

Benefits of Meditation – 159

Meditation Handbook Summary – 160
Relaxed Awareness – 160
Focused Awareness – 162
Uninterrupted Awareness – 165

My Current Practice – 166

Dedication

I dedicate my *Spiritual Autobiography and Meditation Handbook* to my dear wife, who sustains me on my spiritual path. She also lovingly edited this volume.

My wife has asked that I not use her name or speak at length about her in my *Spiritual Autobiography and Meditation Handbook.* I have complied with her wishes.

She feels that this book is my story of my individual spiritual journey. My wife adds, however, that she would be glad to be featured in a different book about our forty-plus years of shared adventures.

"Let your innate urge to be Self- and God-realized inspire your thoughts and actions and direct your path in life." (Roy Eugene Davis)

Spiritual Autobiography and Meditation Handbook

©2014 Emerson Dean Brooking, Ph.D.

Introduction

I have attempted in this *Spiritual Autobiography and Meditation Handbook* to describe my spiritual path. It is the journey from identifying myself as a separate body-mind-personality self to experiencing my essential Self as an expression of Infinite Consciousness-Existence. This *Spiritual Autobiography and Meditation Handbook* describes how I gradually learned how to explore layer, beneath layer, beneath layer of my mind and being – sometimes referred to as "peeling the onion."

My *Spiritual Autobiography and Meditation Handbook* is also a manual. It contains sufficient information and techniques to allow the reader to begin a personal meditation practice. Through God's grace, this intensive meditation practice may lead serious truth seekers to Self- and God-realization.

Over the years, my meditation practice has proven to be Divine Psychotherapy. In these pages, I have shared how I learned to move from the False Self (the self developed in my own likeness rather than in the likeness of God) to the True Self (the image of God in which every human being is created). It has been, and continues to be, a journey teaching me how to relax and learn to "let go and let God."

Childhood

My family numbered seven – my parents, two sets of twins, and my mother's mother, whom I called "Nannie." I was the youngest child in my family, having been born some ten minutes after my sister.

Reverend Cato Dick From birth to age fifteen, I attended Trinity Methodist Church in Chattanooga, Tennessee. This church played a central role in my spiritual development, especially during the years that Rev. Cato Dick was pastor.

Rev. Cato Dick gave an inspiring series of sermons covering his life and ministry that led me to want to be a minister. Indeed, for the first fifteen years of life, I only wanted to be one thing when I grew up – a Methodist minister.

When I was seven years old, I began keeping a journal, a record of personal activities, reflections, and feelings. At that time, I ended each entry with this declaration: "I want to serve you, God!" I also included the total number of sins committed that day, followed by "I hope no more."

(Throughout my life I have continued to periodically maintain a journal. This practice has allowed me to assemble this book from my many writings through the years.)

Practice for the Ministry On Sundays, my family went out to lunch after church. I always ordered fried chicken because I considered it part of my training as a Methodist minister. Ministers were often invited into families' homes for dinner, and in the South they were usually served fried chicken.

I slept on the top bunk and attached a picture of Jesus to the ceiling above me. For years this picture of Jesus was the first thing I saw when I woke up and the last thing before I fell asleep. Each day I would sing, pray, and talk to Jesus. In essence, twice each day I created my own private worship service. During these years, I developed a loving relationship with my Lord, Jesus Christ. This intimate relationship brought me profound peace and joy.

When I was in the sixth grade, my teacher allowed me to teach the Christmas story and to give a test on the material. This experience solidified my desire to be a Methodist minister, teaching about God and leading souls to God.

Adolescence

When I was fifteen, I moved to Atlanta, Georgia. There I went before the Quarterly Conference of my new church and was nominated for my preacher's license. Later, I wrote the following:

The Secret of Happiness

Many people believe that happiness is something you search for, but in the Bible we read the following: "Seek ye first the kingdom of God, and   His righteousness; and all these things shall be added unto you."

The first step toward true happiness is humbling yourself before God, and confessing that you, like so many others, need guidance and forgiveness. "A broken and contrite heart, oh God, thou wilt not despise."

Next, live a surrendered life and try to produce the fruits of the spirit, which are "love, joy, peace, long suffering, gentleness, goodness, faith, meekness, and temperance."

The last and most important step toward happiness is prayer. Prayer relieves your mind from the rush of our modern day. Without prayer you can never be completely happy.

Be at ease with God, for in Him you can rejoice and be exceedingly glad.

This captures the heart of my faith and understanding at age fifteen. The theology I learned in church was very fundamentalist in nature, which would prove to have negative consequences for my later development. Indeed, in time, "my karma ran over my dogma."

Molestation Later that year, my church youth group was involved with six other church youth groups in a revival program. The minister leading this program invited me to come with him and two boys from other churches while they traveled the country for three weeks.

Unfortunately, the minister was a sexual predator, a pedophile. He molested all three of us during the trip. His actions as a man of God created in me massive confusion, anger, and despair. This betrayal of faith haunted me for years, created much anger, and led me to deny God's existence. It was only many years later that I began to heal from this experience.

Education as Key to Peace and Happiness The molestation, angst of puberty and adolescence, Vietnam War, Freedom Movement, drug culture, hippies, and a general distrust of the Establishment – all combined to lead me to abandon my goal of becoming a Methodist minister. Instead, I turned to the accumulation of knowledge and education, which I hoped would bring me peace and happiness.

My new goal was to be a college professor. Eventually, I earned my masters and doctorate degrees, but still was not happy or peaceful.

Introduction to Meditation

In 1985, during a year-long journey around the world, my wife and I traveled to Chaing Mai in northern Thailand. During the afternoon of June 17th, we walked around several wats (Buddhist temples) enjoying the often gaudy colors, incredible carvings, paintings, and statues. One temple, Wat Srigeat, sparkled beautifully in the sunlight filtering through the big trees on the wat grounds. We went in for a closer look and some pictures.

Meeting the Monk After a few minutes, a monk in the standard orange costume stood, waved his hand, and said, "Come over so I can practice my English." His name was Phra. Songdej Dhammatharo. ("Phra." is a title of honor.) He had taught himself English and seemed to have a fair vocabulary, using English words like "delusion." But communication was difficult as the monk did need a lot more practice.

Whenever my wife or I used the word "wonderful," the monk giggled and repeated the word. "Wonderful" became his new favorite word and he started using it in his conversations. Another of the monk's favorite verbalizations was the sentence "Mai Pen Rai" – "It doesn't matter" – a very Buddhist and Thai sentiment.

The three of us sat together beneath one of the big old trees and talked for some twenty-five minutes. Then the monk called to a passing novice and asked him to fetch a key to the "bot" (central sanctuary in a Thai temple). The novice bowed deeply to the monk, showing him great respect.

After going inside the bot and sitting near the five hundred year old Buddha image, we talked together for another hour and a half. The conversation centered on Buddhism, Thai and American culture, and Christianity. The monk also spoke candidly about his interaction with "Life" – men, women, drugs, alcohol, dancing, the way of the world, etc.

He invited us to his room to talk further, and we sat together for another hour or so. The thirty-three-year-old Phra. Songdej told us that he had been a novice from age ten to twenty-one, when he became a monk.

At his request, I pasted our calling card in his address book. When he noticed that I had a Ph.D., he laughed happily, and addressed me as "Dr. Emerson." His address book contained the names of people from all over the world. He said he wanted to come to America someday, but acknowledged the ticket would cost a great deal.

At my request, we meditated together, and I was immediately impressed with the degree of concentration and depth of trance he obtained in a brief period of time. His breathing became very shallow and he almost fell over as he meditated sitting in the lotus position. It reminded me of the deep trance states I had obtained in hypnosis with my clients, although I could not hypnotize myself so quickly or so deeply. At that point in my life, I required another person, an external force, to obtain such a deep trance.

From observing his meditation, I was convinced that hypnosis and meditation were similar processes. The monk told me that he sometimes played a meditation tape to assist him in reaching a deeper level, much as I might use relaxation and induction tapes for hypnosis.

(Over the years, as I have learned more and experienced deeper meditative states, I now believe that there are important differences between meditation and hypnosis. Hypnosis does not postulate that a moral foundation is necessary for success, nor does hypnosis entertain the goal of Self- and God-realization. Success in meditation is unlikely without a strong moral foundation – adhering to the *yamas* and *niyamas*. And the ultimate goal of meditation is Self- and God-realization.)

Using metaphors to explain meditation, the monk held a pencil and noted that most people concentrate on the outside of the pencil, which is painted and an illusion. Some people move to the wood; few achieve the center, the lead. He explained that he seeks the center.

"Concentration is the key!" He added that his formal meditation practice was only one part of concentration. He was one with everything he did – drinking (he drank water to illustrate), eating, walking (he walked in a slow, determined, mindful walk for us), etc.

He shook the glass of water to show how life was agitation. "No one can be centered who is agitated," he declared. "For this reason monks don't touch females as females are filled with electricity." (He grabbed my arm hard and shook it!)

When I asked him to teach me how to meditate, the monk told me he would have to seek permission from his "teacher," the abbot of many wats in the region around Chaing Mai, including Wat Srigeat. His name was Phra. Khru Khantayaporn.

My wife and I had entered Wat Srigeat soon after 2:00 p.m. and left soon after 5:00 p.m. It was a wonderful experience – quite exciting and exotic. The monk invited us to come back to observe evening worship services and meditate together.

Return Visits to Wat Srigeat Later that evening we arrived at the temple for the monks' and novices' evening prayers. After we removed our shoes and put them on a small stand by the door, we visited with Phra. Songdej in his room. Phra. Songdej's little room, his only personal space, was filled with an assortment of stuff – lots of books and everything from glue to a jar of onions preserved in honey. His bed was just a cloth on the floor, with no cushioning.

When the temple bell sounded, we walked down the corridor to a meeting room with a large Buddha image in front. My wife and I sat in the very back and three monks sat in front on a slightly raised stage-like projection near the Buddha image. Eight novices sat between us and the monks. Their chanting was quite beautiful.

The abbot was not present as he was visiting hill tribe temples. I was surprised by the lack of formality; everyone behaved naturally through the chanting. Novices left the room and returned again, seemingly whenever the spirit moved them. One monk read a newspaper through most of the ceremony, though he did lay it aside during the quiet meditation.

Phra. Songdej led much of the chanting. At one point he forgot the words, laughed, and stopped to find the lesson in his book before resuming.

Temple dogs wandered in and out at the doorway, occasionally sitting down to listen for a moment. Lizards ran up and down the walls, often chirping out with their strange cries.

All in all, it seemed an informal and individual gathering – very much like the four clocks hanging at various points around the room, each set to slightly different times and chiming in with pleasant tones just whenever. (I later noted that, when the abbot returned to evening worship, the atmosphere was more formal.) After chanting and reciting, the monks and novices moved off their knees, assumed a lotus position, and meditated.

When the service ended, the novices scattered off and Phra. Songdej called us to the front to chat with him and another monk. We asked Phra. Songdej if we had done anything wrong or inappropriate. He obviously knew the words but seemed unable to process the question, and we never really got an answer.

After reading and learning more about Buddhism, we discovered that several things we did were wrong and inappropriate, from sitting in an equal rather than inferior position to pointing at the Buddha image with our left hand. The left hand is considered unclean, as it is used to wash oneself after a bowel movement, while the right hand is pouring water.

Thai monks were in a status position superior to almost all others and due great respect, even from the king. The monks were being very flexible and understanding of our cultural ways, which were often so much at odds with their own.

Phra. Songdej invited us to return to evening worship the next night if we wished. He also invited me to come at ten the next morning for a photography session, as I had asked him for a time when I could take his picture. Very tired, we mentioned at 8:30 p.m. that we needed to go eat supper. That did not seem to process.

At ten the next morning I had a photography session with Phra. Songdej; I took his picture and he took mine. The monk shared that it was the first time he had ever held a camera.

Several times Phra. Songdej had shown me the meditation technique he used to achieve good meditation. He did so again that morning. As he explained his technique to me, I knew I was missing a lot of significant information. If his English were better and my sensitivity more keen, I would have been able to learn much more from him.

That evening my wife and I returned to Wat Srigeat for evening worship. While in Phra. Songdej's room, he offered us a cookie. After meditation, the novices brought us fruit and some potato chip like snack. Our comment the night before about having no supper must, after all, have made a real impression because suddenly everyone wanted to make sure we had enough to eat.

This concern was seen to be even more gracious when we later learned that monks are allowed to eat only between dawn and noon each day. We also learned that all food in the wat was donated by people in the community.

Meeting the Abbot The next night I went alone to evening worship services. As the abbot had returned to Wat Srigeat and was in conference, services took place in an upstairs room. Phra. Songdej introduced me to his teacher, the abbot, when services ended. His name was Phra. Khru Khantayaporn. The sixty-seven-year-old abbot of Wat Srigeat was also Chief Priest of

Sanpatong. No *farang* (foreigner of European descent) had ever asked him to teach meditation, yet he readily agreed to teach me. He had a pleasant smile and spoke with a soft voice.

The abbot spoke no English, but, using Phra. Songdej as interpreter, talked with me about meditation and began to explain the meditation technique. Unfortunately, the monk was not the best interpreter, so I missed much that the abbot said. I simply could not understand and my monk did not have the skills to explain it more clearly.

My understanding was helped some by the fact that Phra. Songdej had described the meditation technique several times in our earlier conversations. However, it was obvious that the abbot felt that there was only <u>one</u> right way to do the meditation technique, and therefore certain elements must be meticulously explained. The abbot's attitude toward teaching the meditation technique was much more serious and exact than Phra. Songdej's, who often replied in response to a question, "Mai Pen Rai" – "It doesn't matter."

My Studies at the Wat On June 20th, for the first time since I began attending evening worship services, the abbot also attended. Once again I sat in the easy posture during the service. I knew that "legs should not be crossed when sitting on the floor in presence of monks. The feet should be tucked away out of sight under the body in the respect position." (Robert and Nanthapa Cooper, *Culture Shock! Thailand ...And How to Survive It*, 1982 Times Books International, Times Center, 1 New Industrial Road, Singapore, 1953, p.15)

However, I could not maintain the respect position for too long as it was <u>very</u> painful for me. I was not very limber and not accustomed to kneeling on hard floors with only a thin mat for a cushion. So I sat in easy posture. During worship service everyone else was in the respect position, with legs tucked under the body. The abbot sat in a chair. I wondered what the abbot thought of me sitting in the easy position instead of the respect position.

Once again I found that the chanting induced a light trance in me; just listening to it felt wonderful! When the chanting ended, all monks and novices looked from the Buddha image to the abbot. They went through the full respect procedure of the triple obeisance. The abbot then began to speak and it was obvious from the beginning that he was talking about me. He pointed at me and kept looking my way as he spoke. He talked for ten minutes and the service ended.

Phra. Songdej motioned me over and my first question was, "What was your teacher talking about?" The monk replied that the abbot was telling the novices how wonderful it was that I would come all the way from America and spend part of my holiday studying about meditation. Meditation, the abbot added, was a good thing, regardless of religion and nationality.

The next afternoon I went to Wat Srigeat and gave Phra. Songdej an English-Thai dictionary and a blank tape. He agreed to tape the evening worship service. In the evening I attended evening worship and afterwards the abbot gave me some fruit and a medallion which had a picture of the large Buddha image in the bot. Apparently, the previous year was the five hundred year anniversary of its creation. Medallions were cast to commemorate the occasion. The abbot also gave me a medallion to give to my wife.

On June 23rd I went alone to the temple for evening worship. That night chanting was in the Chaing Mai language, which was the original language of this part of Thailand and much faster than the Pali language chanting I had heard during previous worship services. As usual, though, I felt very peaceful and calm after hearing the chanting.

Later, the abbot, with Phra. Songdej as translator, gave more instruction. He carefully reviewed each step of the meditation technique, going into specifics on the order, the sequence used. (Later, I will provide a detailed description of the meditation technique.)

As I had been practicing the technique for many days, I had several specific questions. Once again I was impressed at the importance the abbot placed on the exact details of the technique, for example, the exact location of the injection process and the crystal as it moved through the body.

The abbot told Phra. Songdej to find the right size box, a needle, and some thread. As it took several minutes for the monk to comply with the request, the abbot and I just sat together, occasionally smiling at each other. I was overwhelmed by a sense of deep, serene peace as I sat in the abbot's presence. When the monk finally returned, the abbot threaded the needle and, using the box to represent my body, demonstrated how I should visualize the cord injecting through my body.

When I asked why the crystal should enter the right nostril for males and the left for females, the monk and abbot talked together for many minutes, often laughing. Eventually the monk turned to me and said, "Men and women are made differently." I certainly lost a <u>lot</u> of information because I did not know the language!

Phra. Songdej had a "friend" prepare drawings of a human form which showed the exact locations where the crystal sat and rotated. The abbot studied these drawings carefully and made corrections on them.

As a result of their many great efforts, I finally felt that I had a good understanding of the meditation technique. Now the challenge was to practice the technique at least daily, and more often if possible.

I found that I was already making progress. I could now sometimes "feel" the crystal as it moved over my body, though I often continued to use the tip of my index fingers or the back of a pencil to help me "feel" the crystal as it moved.

I was also really enjoying the sensations produced when the crystal sat at my "third eye", the point between my eyebrows. (This point is also sometimes called the "spiritual eye" or "Christ center.") Its warmth seemed to actually cleanse and purify. It was as though the crystal was opening, expanding my mind, my consciousness – a very powerful sensation!!!

Humbled and feeling quite blessed, I left the wat that evening knowing that I was very fortunate to have been accepted as the abbot's first *farang* student.

For the next several nights I attended evening worship at the temple. During the days I went to the American Information Service Library and read about Buddhism. Every day I meditated, sometimes two and three times during the day. I was beginning to understand more fully the techniques taught by the abbot and monk. It was a very powerful meditation technique, and, if I could master it, I anticipated much reward.

"Concentration" was the most important part of this mastery. "The mind is like a wild car; concentration is the brake," Phra. Songdej would wisely advise. Unfortunately, concentration was hard for me to achieve. The monk encouraged me by saying that it took much practice.

Graduation and a Buddha Image On July 3rd, after evening worship, I went upstairs with Phra. Songdej to meet with the abbot in his living area. I had never been taken there before. The abbot had prepared a handwritten letter and he reviewed it with Phra. Songdej. Leaving the abbot and I alone, the monk took the letter downstairs to type.

The abbot's letter would hopefully help me gain permission from the authorities in Bangkok to send a Buddha image to America. Actually, this Buddha image gift had been talked about several times over many days, so whether it would actually be presented to me was uncertain. Also, once I was given the Buddha image, I was not sure I would be able to get it out of the country. Thailand was <u>very</u> strict about their Buddha images and prohibited their exportation.

(Buddha images are not "idols;" they do not represent any god. They are only an aid to help on the path to enlightenment. While I felt I would like to use the Buddha image as an inspiration in meditation and would enjoy having such a souvenir of our time here, "it doesn't matter," to quote Phra. Songdej's most used phrase. What I had gained was not material, could not be taken away. It remained deep in my soul forever.)

While we waited, I had a <u>wonderful</u> time reviewing the meditation technique with the abbot, mostly nonverbally as I did not speak Thai, Chaing Mai, or Pali, and the abbot did not speak English. The abbot once again examined the diagrams drawn to show the different locations on the body used as focal points in meditation, and revised them in several places to more accurately reflect the correct locations. After demonstrating these, he went through the entire procedure while I followed him. We then meditated together for several minutes.

I enjoyed meditating with the abbot. Just as I had been with the monk, I was most impressed with the ease in which the abbot was able to achieve a deep meditative state. I felt so **GOOD** when our meditation session was over!!! So peaceful and light-hearted did I feel; I thought I could walk on air!

When Phra. Songdej returned with a typed copy of the abbot's letter, the abbot was displeased because his seal was not on the letterhead. The monk then asked if I could return to the wat the next morning to pick up the Buddha image, take pictures of the abbot, and get the letter. Of course, I readily agreed.

Quoting from some material I had been reading: "The impermanence of the world, the lack of any reality based on outward appearances, lead the Buddhist to tolerance. In the midst of this fluidity, in which it would be absurd to wish to establish certainties, exactitude, or planned action, only the present and immediate count... ." (*Guide to Thailand*, Achille

Clarac, ed., translated by Michael Smithies, Oxford University Press, Singapore, 1981)

I then repeated after Phra. Songdej the Five Precepts (all Buddhists to abstain from destroying life, stealing, committing adultery, telling lies, and drinking intoxicating liquors or taking drugs) in Pali language and then repeated after the abbot, who held a fan over his face as was the custom. I'm sure my Pali was the absolute worst they ever heard, but as usual they were very gracious and kind. I felt it was a bit like a graduation exercise – very SPECIAL!!!

[Abbot's Letter]
Wat Srikird
Muang District, Chaing Mai
July 3, 1985

Subject: Donation of "SINGHA I" – a brass Buddha Image
To: Mr. Emerson D. Brooking

I, Prakru Khantayaporn, Wat Srikird Abbot, was pleased that Mr. Emerson believes in Buddhism. He came to Chiang Mai and spent many consecutive days studying and practicing Buddhanusati, "Buddho," meditation. To strengthen his faith in Buddhism, Wat Sridird is pleased to give him a 5" based brass Buddha image for worshiping in Georgia, USA.

Wishing you a safe and sound journey back to your country. Be free from all unhappiness, sorrow, sickness and trouble. Be happy and remain firm with Buddhism forever.

Bless you
Prakru Khantayaporn
Wat Srikird Abbot/Chief Priest of Sanpatong
Wat Srikird   Tel: 221046

On the morning of July 4th, I returned to the wat and took pictures of the abbot and monk. The monk also took my picture as the abbot gave me the Buddha image.

Later, while visiting a bookstore, I met a *forang* monk from Canada, Phra. Brian, who had been a monk for seven months. He emphasized that an English speaking monk was crucial to learning meditation, and, just from our few moments together, I saw how much more I could learn. It was very exciting for me!

I wondered if I could study with an English speaking teacher before I left Thailand. I worried that the state of Georgia in America might be a hard place to find a competent meditation teacher. Phra. Brian said there were about fifty English speaking monks in Thailand. In the evening I returned to the wat for chanting and meditation.

On July 10th I attended my last worship service at Wat Srigeat. Afterwards, I showed Phra. Songdej how to clean his tape player and he gave me a tape of morning worship. As I left, I wondered if I would ever see him or the abbot again.

At the time, it was difficult for me to fully appreciate that a very powerful, life changing event had occurred. Entering Wat Srigeat on June 17th had opened a new world for me – the world of meditation. I did know that I would never forget the hours we spent together, and the many kindnesses both he and the abbot had shown me.

Bangkok, Thailand

My wife and I immediately traveled to Bangkok and I began the process of having the Buddha image approved to leave the country. While I waited, I located Phra. Brian. He was living in his teacher's room in a local wat. His teacher, Phra. George, was in England, and, over a period of five days, Phra. Brian spent many hours with me discussing meditation and Buddhism.

During my first visit to his wat, I walked by a large room and saw a female walking <u>very</u> slowly, so slowly, gracefully, mindfully, that she was actually hypnotic to observe. I found myself relaxing just by watching her. Unfortunately, she eventually noticed my long stare, and I left immediately so she could continue her walking meditation in private. (I did not know it at the time, but I was watching the mindful walking form of vipassana meditation. In a year, I, too, would be practicing vipassana.)

When Phra. Brian offered to supervise me in a ten day, silent vipassana retreat, I was excited and ready to begin. However, my wife was very annoyed when I suggested I check into the wat for ten days, especially when I told her I could have no contact with her, even by telephone. I offered to get her settled in a nicer hotel than the dump we were currently in, but she declared she would rather leave and go back home to America. She began making plans to do so.

She was tired and had a right to be so. I had left her alone for many hours, both in Chaing Mai and Bangkok, in order to learn about and experience meditation. Plus, we had been traveling for almost nine months without rest.

In order to save money, we had mostly camped for a month in Hawaii, in Australia for two months, and in New Zealand for two months. Before we hit Asia, we sent our camping gear home. We then traveled for almost two months in Hong Kong and China. China had just recently opened its borders to independent travelers, and almost no one spoke English. This made doing anything extremely difficult! And recently we had been in Thailand almost two months. As I said, my wife had a right to be tired.

After due consideration, however, especially since Phra. Brian was thinking of leaving Bangkok, it did not seem like a good time for a long retreat. But I resolved to do one later when the opportunity arose.

Actually, I think my wife sensed that, if I did my ten day retreat, she might lose me for ten months or ten years, or even longer. It was obvious that I felt I had discovered a precious gem, meditation, and was eager to immerse myself and go wherever it took me. Her strong reaction to my proposed retreat helped to keep me grounded in our current realities.

When the Buddha image was finally approved for mailing out of the country, we sent it on its way. After an all-night, very uncomfortable train ride, we took a boat to Koh Samui and eventually settled on Lamai Beach.

Koh Samui, Thailand

Koh Samui was a nice rest for both of us and we were able to enjoy a respite from foreign cultures. While there, it often seemed as though we were in Florida or on the Gulf Coast of America, due to the serene, soothing universality of the ocean and beach.

Our bungalow was cool, breezy, had a bathroom, and there was a mosquito net over the bed. A porch overlooked the shore, and was some twenty steps from the Gulf of Siam, with Vietnam and Cambodia beyond. Waves lapped up on the shore with a very pleasant, restful sound.

We had electric lights from 6:00 p.m. to 11:00 p.m. The manager, armed with a pistol, patrolled the compound throughout the night, so we felt pretty safe and secure.

We enjoyed several days of sunshine and collected lots of beautiful shells. I snorkeled daily on a lovely coral reef, which was only a ten minute walk along the shore. We had shady palm trees, complete with the occasional thud of a coconut, and good food at the restaurant. Koh Samui turned out to be paradise!

Excellent drugs were provided by the restaurant/bar. I had never visited any place where drugs were so cheap, so easily available, including some great brownies laced with hashish. Drugs were illegal in Thailand, but, apparently, on Koh Samui drug laws were not strictly enforced.

Actually, consuming dope was a little risky, as "fines for even the smallest amounts of *ganja* are very high – 50,000 Baht ($2,000US) for a couple of grams is not unusual. Those who cannot afford to buy out of this game go to jail." (Joe Cummings, *Thailand – A Travel Survival Kit*, Lonely Planet Publications, P.O.Box 88, South Yarra, Victoria 3141, Australia, 1984, p.113)

Early in our stay on Koh Samui, I ate a hashish brownie and walked down the beach. With each step I got higher and higher. Soon I met an attractive woman who agreed to snorkel naked with me. I found it all very exciting!

But, actually, I did not want to have sex with her. I could not see any sense in possibly messing up my relationship with my wife. After all, I had been married since 1972, and had never committed adultery. Why would I want to start now?

Just days earlier, during the ceremony granting me the Buddha image, I had promised to follow the Buddhist precepts. I also remembered that adultery was forbidden in the Jewish *Torah,* Christian *Bible,* The Buddhist's Precepts, Hinduism, Yoga's y*amas*, the *Qur'an–* all the major religions and spiritual paths. As the *Qur'an* stated, "You shall not commit adultery; it is a gross sin, and an evil behavior." (*Qur'an 17:32)*

And I knew that, if I committed adultery, the guilt and lies would have an extremely negative impact on my spiritual life, my developing meditation practice. I began to realize something quite profound during those days on Koh Samui. Through my meditations I had found my peace within, the Kingdom of God, and I wanted to make protecting my peace my highest priority.

So perhaps the Ten Commandments should not be called "Commandments" at all? Instead, they should be called the "The Ten Paths to Peace and Joy!"

My meditations left me high, but were not illegal, did not cost money, and did not sometimes lead to extreme paranoia. Drugs were illegal, cost money, and often led to paranoia.

Practicing the meditation technique left me with many of the same feelings I had when I used drugs to get high. And, as I played with these discoveries, I found I could not meditate when I was stoned; my concentration was way too scattered. I had to choose between drugs and meditation, which meant that I had to choose between drugs and God. **With great joy I chose God!!!**

I was actually shocked to discover that I preferred meditation over drugs! Here I was in a drug paradise, naked women and all, and I would rather be meditating! It was not a familiar state of mind; it was not an attitude I was comfortable with. It was a little frightening, scary, and it was profoundly **new and exciting**!!!

One evening four beautiful Swedish girls were dropping psychedelic mushrooms and asked me to join them. Ordinarily, I would have jumped at such a heavenly opportunity! But I knew that, if I took a trip, I would feel like hell for days, which would negatively impact the depth of my meditations, negatively impact my ability to enter into the Kingdom of God within me.

So I actually declined the offer to trip with them, and instead declared that I would be their "kite man" if they needed me. Sure enough, when the lights went off at eleven, one of the girls freaked out. As I tried to help her stay half sane, I realized that, if I had ingested the drugs, it could easily have been me, decompensating there on the beach. I was extremely thankful for my developing meditation practice!

Koh Samui was a pleasant interlude and we would have stayed longer, but our visas were about to expire. Malaysia, Singapore, India, Greece, Egypt, and Israel lay ahead!

Buddhist or Christian? – Penang, Malaysia

Our stay in Penang, Malaysia allowed me the opportunity to further consider if I should become a Buddhist. I no longer called myself a Christian, but would only say that I was raised in the Christian church. Actually, I did not call myself anything anymore. Should I then become a Buddhist?

I liked Buddhism's emphasis on individual responsibility; people were responsible for their own behavior, their own karma. Our actions produced good, bad, or neutral karma. Of course, I continued to have a problem understanding chance misfortunes, but then I had never been happy or satisfied with <u>any</u> explanations for these.

Life was *dukkha* (unsatisfactoriness, suffering), resulting from my desires (*tanha*) to have or not have. Release from desire leads to release from *dukkha*, release from suffering. I <u>liked</u> these ideas; they had great appeal to me; they struck me as sound and true!

As I struggled with ideas, I could see why there was much that attracted me to Buddhism. Nothing had to be accepted on faith; there was no Apostles' Creed, no virgin birth, no resurrection from the dead, etc., etc. There was only what could be judged using a critical eye.

And yet Buddhism encompassed beliefs that could not be "proven." Who could prove that we are born again in <u>any</u> other life?! And, yet, even if there were no other heaven or hell or rebirth or chance to achieve nirvana, I <u>liked</u> the Buddhist tenet which held that, as the world <u>is</u> full of suffering, one should in no way add to this vast storehouse of suffering.

I had tried to live my life without causing pain to others. Indeed, I gained pleasure and satisfaction as I thought of the jobs I previously had and the ways which I had used those positions to benefit others. Human service jobs gave me a chance to provide human service!!!

But then Buddhism was a somber, "depressing" religion. To be a Buddhist, I must relinquish the notion of having an immortal soul, that is, the notion that I have a self, a permanent identity. Buddhism held that the person, Emerson Dean Brooking, was just a conglomeration of senses – seeing, hearing, touching, smelling, tasting, and thinking – nothing more, just the sum of these.

Buddhism further held that everything passed away, that Emerson Dean Brooking changed from minute to minute. The Emerson Dean Brooking of five minutes ago was not the Emerson Dean Brooking of the present moment. Actually, I too believed that everything passed away. "The essence of all things is fire; you cannot step into the same river twice." (Heraclites) But giving up the idea of having an immortal soul went contrary to much of my lifelong beliefs.

> ... what passes on – up or down, so to speak – is a small, constantly changing part of a very large Karmic force, and not recognizable personality. Buddha himself denied the existence of an immortal soul, and even produced thirty-two beliefs concerning it, all of which he believed to be wrong. This statement, or part of it, was subsequently extended into the rigid 'Anatman' doctrine of the Theravada School, who maintained – to their great loss as far as public appeal was concerned – that words such as 'personality,' 'ego,' and 'immortal soul' had no meaning whatever in the scheme of future existences. Criticized as one of the more depressing dogmas of Buddhist teaching, this has never had a widespread understanding or appeal ... .(*Buddhism In Malaya*, Colin McDougall, 1956, Donald Moore Publishers, Singapore)

While I embraced much of Buddhism, I resolved to never forget my Christian roots! Christianity taught me to care, to love others, to treat others as I, too, would like to be treated. My early loving relationship with Jesus Christ had set the foundation for my life, and influenced my educational and vocational goals.

I concluded my inquiry into whether I should become a Buddhist by deciding not to decide, to continue considering it as my meditation practice deepened.

Months later my wife and I returned home. I had faithfully continued my meditation practice throughout this time, but found that I was not experiencing the dramatic progress I experienced in the beginning. I feared that the "honeymoon period" had ended. I wrote a letter to Phra. Brian telling him of my progress and asking for his advice. His response was edifying:

A Monk's Letter

January 11, 2529

Dear Emerson,

Received your letter this morning before breakfast when I descended from the new little house they've built for me up on the high hill out back. I am happy that you got the letter and books without any problem. The same day you returned – hunh! I bet that tickled.

You write "Life in America has hit me full in the gut. Daily hassles seem more than I can cope with at times." I may have said to you that, when one visits Third World countries with their 'slower pace of living,' the problem that faces the First World traveler isn't culture shock but re-culture shock when he returns to what is supposed to be familiar society. Of course, your resolve to practice meditation on a regular basis, even though you don't feel it will be an in-depth pursuit due to limited amounts of time, is the sanest approach. To just allow space in personal relationships will help you to maintain balance. …

You are back in a very intensive part of the world where the pressure to homogenize is probably the greatest anywhere. At least much more so than that as a budget traveler where absolutely none exists and it isn't expected because you're "just passin' thru... ." ... Your opinion of the world is what creates the world as such for you and, as such, you create your own reality moment to moment and must accept responsibility for it. If I may, it sucks everywhere. I wish you the best of smooth success in handling it. ...

I am glad to hear that you have continued your meditation. You write, "I do not feel I have made much progress," All I can say is take heart. You continued with "I do find that, even on bad days, I feel better after meditation than before. This encourages me to continue." It works like that. This is the importance of meditation; not the psychedelic effects which are non-applicable to everyday existence, but the effects which one takes with one out of the session. These are almost always more subtle but are what count in this game, The Final Game.

Seeing as how happiness has very little to do actually with pleasure but mostly with victory, it is the hardest things in life to win which count for the most. The conquest of that which has been termed "the forest monkey mind" is the hardest to win, the most worthwhile, and the struggle for which can be counted on to throw up the most traumas along the way. Life would be charmless without challenges. How would you like your steaks thrown into a blender and strained for you?

A rough meditation session is indicative of progress for vipassana, insight meditation. Because the signs of progress appear in the mundane sphere, a teacher can often tell when a student has made progress whereas the student will think that he is doing worse.

The technique which you are practicing utilizing the concept of the crystal is a Samadhi technique. As we discussed, this is serenity meditation, which is where the so-called psychedelic effects are bound to occur the strongest. In fact, they are to be grabbed and increased by the practitioner to complete absorption strength until only the effect is there and all thought pattern has ceased. When one reads, cogitates on and absorbs the Buddha's teaching, one progresses on the path of vipassana anyways. There is an old saying that Samadhi develops panna (wisdom) and panna develops Samadhi.

… Without an experienced teacher you will find that your practice will turn up wavering effects from signs of progress in one of the fields to the other. Do keep at it. As the old saying related above expounds, the two do lean up against each other.

If I may advise, seeing as how your time for practice is limited and the demands of your daily living being what they are, it would be more beneficial at this point to continue with a practice of Samadhi (serenity/concentration) as it will give you a pleasant break from the pressures of the workaday world. It will also enhance your ability to concentrate on your affairs, although both would do this, but from different angles.

In the Samadhi, just a couple of hours a day are enough to make progress noticeable to the practitioner. For the vipassana, an intensive period of exclusive training is desirable. Try to maintain mindfulness of thought and present action all day long.

If I may advise with some technical advice based on what you have written about, you write, "The 'third eye' location continues to be very powerful for me. Perhaps it is here that I generate more alpha waves." It was in light of your last mention to me of effects in this area that I sent the instructions I did. Be careful of discursive thought during the practice as to why what is happening is. This will only take you away from the main and useful subject of meditation. …

… So, all my best; my, but I have gone on here. Fond regards to your wife (hmmm… is such proper terminology for a monk?). I guess I should do something "priestly" besides just wish you good health and happiness, so …

Blessings from wherever you've earned them,
Your friend in truth,
Pra. Brian Sannacitto

Introduction to Serenity Meditation

Adopting Pra. Brian's term, I called this meditation technique the "Serenity Meditation" because its use often left me feeling tranquil and serene. The profound peace and joy were similar to that which I experienced as a child and as a youth during my loving relationship with my Lord, Jesus Christ.

I so desired this peace and joy, which I experienced while practicing the Serenity Meditation, and found it supremely ironic that the answers I had been seeking my entire life were within me the whole time.

Occasionally, I have been asked to teach the Serenity Meditation. I am pleased to do so and only ask that the person practice the technique for a month, at least once a day for a minimum of twenty minutes. I have become convinced that the Serenity Meditation can be useful for all people, irrespective of their religious beliefs or lack thereof.

Because I wanted this meditation technique to appeal to a wide audience, I stripped the technique of its Buddhist concepts. However, there may be some Buddhists, and others, who will want to know what these concepts are. The abbot called this technique Buddhanusati, "Buddho," meditation. According to the monk, some of the Buddhist concepts include the following:

1. Nine circles – eight times represent the Eightfold Path (Right Understanding, Right Thought, Right Speech, Right Action, Right Means of Livelihood, Right Endeavor, Right Mind Control, and Right Meditation), and the ninth Nirvana.

2. Three circles – once for the Buddha, once for the Dharma (law), and once for the Sangha (order of monks).

3. As the crystal enters the nostril, silently repeat "Buddho, Buddho, Buddho."

The following is my summary of the Serenity Meditation. If anyone practicing this technique has questions, please feel free to contact me.

Serenity Meditation Instructions

Imagine a round crystal (or, if you prefer, a small cross) which is very clear, warm, and bright, and which has brilliant light waves emanating from it. As you direct the path of the crystal around and through your body, feel it illuminating and cleansing both your mind and your body, leaving you with a profound sense of tranquility. All movement of the crystal should be very slow and deliberate, and all circles are clockwise.

The mind is like a caged drunken monkey, stung by a scorpion, dashing and darting about from one thought to another. Concentration on the crystal acts as a "brake" on the mind and empties the mind of other thoughts. In addition, the crystal illuminates and cleanses both mind and body.

Path of crystal is as follows:

1. Start at your umbilicus (navel) and circle 9 times.

2. Move up to your xiphoid [xiphisternum – the small extension of the lower part of the sternum (chest bone) between the ribs] and circle 3 times.

3. Do figure eights around your breasts 3 times.

4. Move up to the sternal notch (jugular notch) and circle 3 times.

5. Move up to your Adams apple and circle 3 times.

6. Move up to your lips and trace their outline 3 times.

7. Move up to your nostrils and trace each nostril opening 3 times, beginning with the right nostril.

8. Move up to your eyes and trace the outline of each eye 3 times, beginning with the right eye.

9. Move up to just above the junction of your eyebrow lines. Circle 3 times, imagining bright red streaks of fire moving from the crystal into the head.

10. Move up to the center of forehead, just below hair line, and circle 3 times. Imagine rays of white light illuminating your brain.

11. Move to the top of head and circle 9 times.

12. Move to occiput (back of head) and circle 3 times.

13. Move down spine to base of spine, directly opposite navel, and circle 3 times.

14. Circle waistline 3 times.

15. Begin moving up from waist on right side of body. Move up to right armpit, down inside of arm, over middle finger, up outside of arm, over shoulder to right ear. Circle right ear 3 times.

16. Move up to top of head and circle 3 times.

17. Move to left ear and circle 3 times.

18. Move over left shoulder, down outside of left arm, over middle finger, up inside of arm to armpit, down left side of body to waist.

19. INJECTION PROCESS -- Imagine injecting a cord through the center of your body, starting on your left side at your waist and moving to your right side. Then imagine injecting a second cord through the center of your body, starting at the navel to your spine.

20. Move crystal up to your nostril. As crystal enters nostril, silently repeat your sacred word or phrase 3 times.
Males: Crystal enters right nostril.
Females: Crystal enters left nostril.

Move crystal inside skull to spot just above junction of eyebrow lines. This is the same position outlined in step #9 except now crystal is inside of body. Once again imagine bright red streaks of fire emanating from the crystal.

21. Imagine the crystal descending through the center of your body, coming to rest at intersection of the two cords, previously mentally created, running perpendicular to each other. This resting point is in the center of your body, a distance of two fingers above your navel. The crystal continues to emanate light rays in all directions. The crystal remains here during meditation. (When I practiced, I found it useful to move the crystal back up to

the position outlined in #20. This position is sometimes called the "third eye" or "Christ Center.")

22. The crystal then moves up through the center of your body and exits through your nostril.
Males: Crystal exits left nostril.
Females: Crystal exits right nostril.

First Vipassana Meditation Retreat

A friend, Robert Wootton, recommended that I go to Southern Dharma, a retreat center located on the side of a North Carolina mountain. I arrived Thursday night just as the teacher, Rodney Smith, and two staff members were leaving to eat dinner in Hot Springs. (Rodney had spent four years in Thailand and Burma practicing vipassana meditation.)

When the work retreat began, Rodney explained the basics of vipassana meditation. During the weekend, I sat in meditation for eight hours and did walking meditation for six hours. Early in the retreat Rodney came by while we were in sitting meditation and straightened my back so that I had a more erect sitting posture. I swore he would not have to do that again and held myself very erect after that.

Indeed, I was so erect that a muscle pulled in my shoulder, between my shoulder blades. This was an old injury which had first occurred while canoeing against the wind in an Everglades trip in 1971. By Saturday night the pain was so great that I had to hold my hands over my head!

My right foot also experienced a great deal of pain. This place where the leg joined the foot was the same spot I had injured when my wife and I left for our trip around the world. This pain would go away when I uncrossed my leg.

This bodily pain was intense, but I was feeling very high and mellow from my meditation. In my teacher interview with Rodney on Saturday, I described to him how, when the retreat began, it took me awhile to get more mellow, but the feeling did eventually come. Rodney became very angry and repeatedly said that he wanted to shake me.

Meditation Not Just Being High – It is Solid! "Meditation is contact with the ground, Emerson; it is not just another form of being high. It is solid!" With that said he looked around for a rock, picked it up and gave it to me saying, "Hold this to remind you how meditation brings solid contact with the earth."

I tried to wash some of the dirt off the rock and laughed at my desire to avoid contact with the soil. But the rock certainly did the trick! (I still have the rock. It sits on my private altar in front of the Buddha image given to me by the monks in Thailand.)

After the interview with Rodney, I became aware of a sense of grief, deep and penetrating. It built during the day and I cried once in the early evening. After the last sitting, when the meditation hall was empty, I walked. I began to cry and cried for a long time – a soundless cry with tears streaming down my face. I washed the floor of the hall with my tears – walking and weeping. I wept for what – I know not. But I wept solidly and utterly.

I did not know where vipassana meditation would lead me from there, but I resolved to continue to practice. It was obviously a powerful practice, opening areas within me I did not know existed.

When I did not have an extended period to practice, I would do the Serenity Meditation. When I had a longer period of time, I would do vipassana meditation, both sitting and walking. Often, when I did vipassana meditation, I would keep Rodney's stone with me. When I walked with it, it weighed a ton. I felt as though the bottoms of my feet might bruise from the weight!

Mindfulness (Vipassana) Meditation Instructions

Introductory Meditation Exercises to Cultivate Presence

(Adapted from a summary by Robert Wootton, Ph.D. Used with his permission. Robert has offered to answer any questions you may have. He may be contacted at rw.home@frontier.com)

Two principles:

(1) There is just what there is. Our task is to know (by direct feeling, not thinking about it) what each moment's experience is. When one sits, stands, or walks, know that there is sitting, standing, or walking. When there is sensation in the body, whether pleasant, unpleasant, or neutral, know that there is pleasant, unpleasant, or neutral sensation. When one sees something, know that there is seeing. When thoughts or visual images appear, know that there is thinking or seeing, without getting lost in the content, story line, or meaning of the thought or vision. When sounds call attention, know that at that moment there is hearing; and, if thoughts or feelings occur about the sound, know that at that moment there is thinking or feeling.

(2) Only the mind that clings to nothing, and is able to both open to and let go of everything, can be fully present and know what there is in each moment. Thus, when a sensation arises, one is willing to experience it as it actually is for as long as it lasts and to let go of it when it changes or ceases. Let go of ideas about how meditation should be and acknowledge what is actually occurring. This direct, non-judgmental contact with experience allows and is a transformation of our normal compulsive manner.

Two occasions for practice:
(1) Sitting: Focus attention on the sensations of breathing wherever it occurs most predominantly, either at the nostrils or in the chest-abdomen area. Allow breathing to occur and change however it will. Feel the sensations of the in-breath or the rising movement, and the sensations of the out-breath or falling movement, however long or short, soft or tense, rhythmic or irregular it may be. Be with the entire duration of each in and out, or rise and fall, noticing the beginning and ending moments. To help maintain focus, make soft mental notes: "in," "out," or "rising," "falling." If sounds, sensations, or thoughts call attention away, experience these with equal attention and note "hearing," "feeling," or "thinking." As soon as sounds, sensations, or thoughts recede, gently return to the sensation of breathing.

If there is discomfort and an impulse to move, notice the feelings and the intention and then move slowly enough to notice the sensations of moving. If drowsiness or nodding occurs, focus attention on those sensations. Do the same for other mental states such as boredom, agitation, etc. Maintain attention on the sensation of breathing as the predominant object of awareness. At whatever point one notices the attention elsewhere, note what is occurring and return to the breath. There is no need for judgment or criticism; but, if they occur, note them also. Do the same also for controlling the breathing.

(2) Walking: Pick a short space in which to walk back and forth. Walk at a slow enough pace to move one foot at a time and distinguish the three parts – lifting, moving, placing. Focus attention on the sensations of each part, however one experiences each in the body. To aid focus, note "lifting," "moving," "placing." The technique is then the same as for sitting. Try to feel directly and in minute detail exactly what the experience of walking and breathing is. The aim is to cultivate the kind of continuous, accurate mindfulness that would allow one to give a summary afterwards of the changing sensations and objects of consciousness that occurred.

Death of "Personal I" – A Dream

Issues arising from my continuing meditation practice began to invade my dream world. On May 23, 1986, I had a dream which I immediately recorded. I remembered being in a panic in the dream. I wanted to become more whole, quieter, and more aware. A guru was saying that "I" would die that way. I protested and said, "But I am meditating daily." She looked very disturbed by this bit of news, shook her head, and walked away. She then stated that I was massively neurotic and ordered that I be removed from the group. The guru insisted that I was too full of cancer. Continuous action with little reflection was the only way to survive.

On July 16th I presented this dream to my Dream Group. I found it very difficult to discuss my dream in the group, but did so, regardless. I thought the old, familiar part of me was dying, and the guru was warning me of its death. My meditation experiences had opened up a part of me that was not a "joiner."

Mine was very much an individual journey. I could now live without wanting to get high or smoke dope or use alcohol. I was more at peace in myself than I had ever been. Drugs were no longer necessary! I was free!

The "cancer" was that I was not a joiner, a "disciple." My way was alone, individual. I could "pollute" others if I remained in the group. I did feel "massively neurotic," laid bare by the meditation practice. I did not know where it was going and feared getting far away from who I had been, but I rejoiced at the possibilities too!

Or was the "cancer" spiritual growth? If so, was it to be feared?

"Meditating daily" – perhaps this was a spiritual warning.

After I presented this dream, the facilitator of my Dream Group telephoned me at home and added this dream interpretation: "Perhaps this dream is warning you because you learned meditation in a non-Christian environment."

Apparently her "spiritual teacher" had her repeat "Blessed is the Father, the Son, and the Holy Spirit" just before she meditated in a non-Christian environment. (I did not tell her that each time, before I meditated, I performed five prostrations in front of my Buddha image, one prostration each for the "Buddha, Dharma, Sangha, Mother and Father, and Teacher.")

When I told Rodney Smith at Southern Dharma about my dream, he suggested that I was experiencing the death of "personal I." The Buddhist Anatman Doctrine of no permanent self was being experienced personally as I became more deeply involved in sitting meditation.

Rodney's dream interpretation helped me understand phenomena that sometimes occurred when I prepared to meditate. I would feel very uneasy, almost scared. I felt my "little self" would have to die if I wanted to join with the "big Self." That is, if the boundaries separating me from all others were to dissolve, the little self had to die. Only then would I experience Self-realization.

Introduction to Progressive Muscle Relaxation

In 1986, I became a college professor, Chair of the Psychology Department. I loved the opportunity to serve the college and surrounding community. That was my ministry!

During my teaching career, I frequently taught Introduction to Counseling. The workbook that accompanied the textbook contained a section on progressive muscle relaxation. I practiced this exercise with my students each time I taught the course.

I was struck with how deeply my students appreciated the opportunity to relax, and how eager they were to learn relaxation skills. Their lives were filled with stress, suffering, unsatisfactoriness, and pain. Deep relaxation allowed them a brief respite and improved their coping skills.

I understood meditation to be a "relaxed, focused, uninterrupted awareness." The ability to relax was, therefore, essential for a productive meditation practice. If the meditator was unable to "let go and let God," little progress would occur.

When I later learned about yoga, I discovered that one approach to *yoga nidra* (deep relaxation) was progressive muscle relaxation. The following is a progressive muscle relaxation routine. In yoga, one starts relaxing at the feet and works up the body to the top of the head. This mirrors yoga's emphasis on encouraging an upward flow of *kundalini,* a flow of energy from the base of the spine to the top of the head.

Progressive Muscle Relaxation Instructions

Progressive muscle relaxation involves learning to tense and release muscle groups throughout the body. The objective is to become more aware of the distinction between tension states and relaxation states, thus providing you with self-control procedures designed to reduce unnecessary anxiety and tension. With practice you will learn to induce total bodily relaxation.

Progressive muscle relaxation is best learned in a quiet setting and in a prone position. Tense each muscle group for five to seven seconds. Then release tension immediately rather than gradually. For thirty to forty seconds, enjoy the feelings in the muscles as they loosen up, smooth out, unwind, and relax more and more deeply. Do one or two tension/release cycles per muscular group, concentrating on the differences between tension and relaxation. Once a muscle group is relaxed, do not move it unnecessarily.

A. Legs and Feet (start with dominant side first, then nondominant side)
1. Push toes toward back wall
2. Pull toes toward head
3. Keeping leg straight, clinch thighs and raise legs and feet a few inches off supporting surface

When you relax, do not slowly lower your leg, nor should you slam it down. Rather, let it fall like a ripe fruit falls from a tree.

Just release it. It is as though your leg is supported by a string, and someone cuts the string and the leg drops.

Very slowly and mindfully, move your foot back and forth, finding a comfortable position, and forget about it. (This "forgetting about it" is an important step to learn. Deep meditation cannot easily occur unless all sense doors have been closed.)

Now do the same procedure for the nondominant hand and arm

B. Buttocks, anus muscles, pelvic area
1. Tighten your buttocks, anus muscles, pelvic area

C. Belly
1. Breathing in through the nostrils, fill up the belly with air. Like blowing up a balloon, blow it up even higher.
2. Open your mouth and let the air gush out! (This is not a quiet out breath.) Imagine all the tension in the body gushing out with the breath.

D. Chest
1. Breathing in through the nostrils, fill up your chest with air
2. Open your mouth and let the air gush out! (Once again, this is not a quiet out breath.) Imagine all the tension in the body gushing out with the breath.

E. Shoulders
1. Lift your shoulders and try to touch your ears
2. Push your shoulders in front of the chest, like you want to touch your shoulders together in front of the chest
3. Push your shoulders down toward your feet, like you want to touch your feet

F. Hands and Arms (start with dominant side)

1. Splay out your fingers
2. Make a fist
3. Keeping your fist, lift your arm and hand a few inches, keeping your arm straight
4. Relax
5. Now slowly roll your hand back and forth, find a comfortable position, and forget about it

G. Neck
1. Lift head just an inch or two and tighten all muscles in neck by pushing chin toward chest, but keeping it from touching chest
2. Relax
3. Now very slowly roll head back and forth. Find a comfortable position and forget about it.

H. Face
1. Bite hard and pull back corners of mouth
2. Open mouth, move jaw up and down and all around
3. Stick out tongue as far as you can
4. Squint eyes and wrinkle nose
5. Lift eyebrows toward forehead
6. Take all the muscles of face and try to touch your nose

After each of the muscle groups has physically been tensed and relaxed once or twice, mentally scan each muscle group throughout your body and let go of any remaining tension. This can be accomplished by breathing in – focusing, and breathing out – relaxing. As you breathe in, you focus on the tension in that area of the body. As you breathe out, you allow that tension to flow out with your out breath.

Now, as you become totally aware of the good feelings of relaxation, warmth, and calmness throughout your body, silently repeat to yourself a sacred word or phrase. With practice you will learn to associate your sacred word or phrase with feelings of calmness and relaxation.

Whenever you find yourself becoming tense or anxious, think of your sacred word or phrase. As you silently repeat it to yourself, feel calmness and relaxation sweeping over your body. When you are relaxed, it is easier to maintain inner balance and stability, and to deal fully and clearly with every situation you face. It also allows you to move more deeply into your meditation practice.

Like all skills, learning to relax takes practice. If you practice relaxing, you will get better at relaxing. It is best to practice with the whole body supported. When we practiced in my classroom, students had to maintain sufficient muscle tension to keep from falling out of their chairs. I will never forget one student who relaxed so deeply she fell out of her desk, and hit the concrete floor with a thud. Thankfully, she was not seriously injured.

Southern Dharma Retreat Center

In July, 1986, I did my second vipassana retreat at Southern Dharma. When the retreat ended, I asked Elizabeth Kent, the Director, if I could stay some additional days. She agreed, and I spent the next few days meditating and copying tapes of Dharma talks.

Retreatants who had attended previous retreats had requested taped copies of the evening Dharma talks. I would copy a Dharma talk for someone else and then make a copy for me. I returned home with a large library of Dharma talks.

I so admired Elizabeth Kent's open heart and generous spirit, and appreciated that Southern Dharma was quickly becoming my "spiritual hospital" – a powerful place for rest, meditation/prayer, and the renewal of my spiritual life.

Southern Dharma Retreat Center is located in the Blue Ridge Mountains of Western North Carolina. Elizabeth Kent, a founder, wrote that Southern Dharma was created from "a rugged, remote 135 acre farm on Hap Mountain in the community of Spring Creek, with a bold rushing creek, a knoll and vistas, huge boulders, fields and forests and ferns – everything that makes the mountains so alluring."

During the next several years I attended many retreats at Southern Dharma. These retreats represented a variety of spiritual approaches, including Buddhist, Christian, Hindu, and Taoist traditions. I will discuss only a few of these.

All Southern Dharma retreats were small and emphasized meditation and silence as ways to cultivate the inner life. Retreats ran from three to ten days. Many years of attending Southern Dharma retreats allowed me to develop a more fruitful foundation for my spiritual practice. See www.southerndharma.org to learn more.

Vipassana Meditation on the Mountain Top

In early October, 1987, I went on my third vipassana meditation retreat, led by John Orr. In the 1970's, John received Theravada Buddhist ordination after training in Thailand and India for eight years.

I spent three days on the mountain – meditating, being – being with myself in vipassana meditation, in mindfulness. The rising and falling of the abdomen – the lifting, moving, placing of the foot. Walking and sitting, walking and sitting.

One guided meditation was the most intense of any I had ever experienced. It made all others seem almost tame. I was <u>with</u> the beginning, middle, and end of the rising of the abdomen. I was <u>with</u> the beginning, middle, and end of the falling of the abdomen.

When "smiling into my body," I began to be stronger in sensation on the "in" breath. I began to see a white light, searing and warm, entering my nostrils, into behind my third eye, filling my head with radiant light. I was then able to sweep my <u>whole</u> body, with the white light exploding out of my feet and toes.

John Orr suggested opening the eyes to let in a bit of light, but, when I opened my eyes, I found the daylight <u>so</u> dark in comparison to this white light filling my <u>entire</u> body!!! It was <u>such</u> a state of ecstasy I cannot even now believe how wonderful was the experience.

After one long sit, John Orr began another chant. I joined in with such a relish. Ecstasy, heat, almost took off the top of my head. We then ended for breakfast. I bowed before the Buddha image five times – to the Buddha, Dharma, Sangha, Mother and Father, and Teacher. I had not done this in months as I had stopped after my second retreat of the summer. After all, I reasoned, why forsake one religion, Christianity, for another, Buddhism? Why not discover <u>complete</u> freedom?!

Anyway, after my five bows I began to weep uncontrollably. I wept from such a deep sorrow. As I moved into a fetal position, lying alone in the meditation hall, I wept <u>so</u> strongly, thoroughly. This is not the first time I have touched such deep sorrow on these retreats. But to have such ecstasy and such sorrow so closely tied <u>was</u> a surprise. They must really be flip sides of the same coin.

Our walk from Southern Dharma to the top of Hap Mountain was splendid. Up we climbed at a steady pace – a glorious climb! And then we sat. I moved apart and put on all my warm gear. I was comfortable! It began to rain just enough to let me feel the rain in my face. Clouds drifted by and I thought of New Zealand – "remembering, remembering." It was such a glorious time! And then I ran down the mountain – all the way! Took a hot shower and had another wonderful meal.

During 1986 I attended four meditation retreats at Southern Dharma Retreat Center. All of them were intensive vipassana meditation experiences. By the end of the year, I had adopted Southern Dharma as my "spiritual hospital" and fully appreciated the power of intensive, mindfulness meditation practice.

Through my vipassana meditation practice, I discovered a deep reservoir of sorrow within me. It was as though I had been stuffing, stifling all negative emotions deep within my heart, and vipassana meditation ripped open my heart, allowing these emotions to manifest. In a real sense, I learned to allow the birth of these emotions. I learned that I would not be destroyed by them.

The Small Heavenly Microcosmic Orbit

In August of 1987, I attended a seven-day Vipassana retreat at Southern Dharma with the meditation teacher, John Orr. On August 12, 1987, and for several days afterwards, I had the most incredible experience – waves of uncontrollable energy that forever shattered my skepticism of that which cannot be seen or proven.

Everyone left the meditation hall at 10:07 p.m. and by 11:03 "the event" was over. While I sat in meditation, large pains came in the right side of my neck and shoulder. (This was the site of a canoeing injury I received during an Everglades trip in 1971.)

Waves came and disappeared. I cried out as each new wave built; then I found myself convulsing as I breathed deeply, very quickly! But the breathing was not forced; it came naturally with the pain. Energy was trying to break through a blockage created by the old injury.

And then I found myself rising off my cushion in a corkscrew fashion, as though exploding. Even the pain in my right leg joined and moved up my body to the top of my head. The corkscrew movement was incredible and I collapsed from exhaustion.

When I recovered, I sat up again. Once again the pain, the convulsions built until I exploded. Again I moved in a corkscrew fashion as I lifted off my cushion. It was a primal birth and such an incredibly powerful experience!!!

I stood up and my whole body was electrified as flashes moved up my leg to the top of my head. It was as though a whole new level of consciousness gripped my being. I walked outside and everything seemed naturally slowed. I was AWAKE! I was awake to everything.

I felt so alive, so awake!

A wave of energy continuously circled my head and torso. Not having any control over it terrified me, and for a while I feared it would never stop. I could not sleep because this flowing energy never abated. Thoughts were continuously racing through my mind. When I tried to practice sitting meditation, I could not stay still on my cushion and I would actually rock back and forth in rhythm to the flow of energy.

John recommended that, for the remainder of the retreat, when everyone else practiced sitting meditation, I should walk. This walking movement would be more consistent with the energy moving through my body. He also recommended a book.

This flow of energy around and around my body continued for several days and finally, slowly diminished. When I returned home, I immediately purchased the book John recommended, *Awaken Healing Energy Through the Tao*, by Mantak Chia (Aurora Press, P.O. Box 573, Santa Fe, New Mexico, 87504, 1983).

As I read the book, I was amazed to find on page 75, Diagram 29, titled "The Microcosmic Orbit." There was a diagram of the energy path I was experiencing, though my energy path only went around the main torso and head, not the legs.

Then on page 149 I found the energy path I was experiencing. This path around the main torso and head was called the "Small Heavenly Cycle (Microcosmic Orbit)."

> When the energy flows into the fetus' body, it enters at that point at which the naval will later be after the umbilical cord is severed. Then it proceeds downwards to the bottom of the trunk, flows all the way up the spine to the crown of the head and from there, flows down the middle of the face continuing on to the navel, again to complete the circuit.

Until this experience, I had always thought of energy flows, chakras, and Kundalini energy as intellectually interesting, but concepts that could not be proven. After this experience, my skepticism was shattered and I was a true believer. These were no longer curious intellectual concepts, but instead my reality.

"Stream Entry" – A Dream and Interpretation

During the night of November 1, 1987, I had a powerful dream which once again captured my continuing issues in my meditation practice. The dream was as follows:

It was like being caught in a large wave of water. It had been raining and the water rose quickly, catching me, lifting me up and taking me down stream. I was very fearful, could not believe "I" was dying. Incredible waves swept me through this narrow canyon. I passed by my brother, who was safe on the shore, and gave him something, asking him to keep it dry and protected. As I disappeared down the river, he winked and smiled. I said, "See you perhaps in another life," and lay back in the water, resigned to the death of "me."

Suddenly I noticed that the canyon opened up, and the river became broader and slower. I could now easily swim to the left side and climb out. I struggled up the shore and onto a table. I fell to my knees and wept like a baby because "I" had been saved. I was aware how stupid I must look as "I" wept on this table, but "I" did not care. "I" did not have to die!!!

Comments The Buddhist Anatman Doctrine held that there was no permanent self, no "I". Each time "I" began my meditations, there was fear because the "I" or independent ego must perish so that merging with God, with the Infinite, became possible. My meditation practice appeared to be a journey over which "I" had no control. That is, "I" seemed to be propelled along with little chance of escape.

The "incredible waves" reminded me of Lava Falls in the Grand Canyon, and how I feared for the safety of those people who were thrown out of the "thrill boat" and caught in the current. All of them survived, as did "I" in my dream.

Perhaps the dream was telling me that, in spite of my fears, "I" could survive my meditation practice! "I" could merge with the infinite, be Self- and God-realized, and remain an individualized unit of God's consciousness. Both were possible!

Overwhelming Sorrow

On Saturday night, May 28, 1988, I was participating in a Southern Dharma retreat with John Orr. As John was leaving the meditation hall (he was the last person to leave), I told him I would turn out the lights.

I sat and within minutes began crying. Large, heaping tears began to flow. I cried out in my pain of sorrow. Trying not to be overwhelmed by fear of the intensity of the experience, I began to be engulfed by wave after wave of sadness. I yelled out in my painful sorrow.

Someone came into the hall. I attempted to quiet myself but tears kept coming. After a couple of minutes, the person rose, came over, hugged me, and departed. I then began to really experience grief. Very loudly I cried out, overcome with pain!

As the intensity grew, I began to feel nauseous. I thought I would become insane – over the edge of sanity – and not recover. Indeed, I was very crazy! For awhile, anyway....

In the height (or depth) of this pain, I felt myself turning like a corkscrew – upward wildly! Then I fell exhausted.

Someone came into the hall and I left. It was 11:30 p.m. when I finally got to my bed. For days afterwards I felt the nausea, the disease, dis-ease. Whenever I sat for more than 20-30 minutes, I began to feel nauseous. I felt differently than I ever had before – more unsure, dis-eased.

But my dream that Saturday night was reassuring, and I slept most peacefully. I dreamed I was bent over and one of my psychology students came by and took my arm and helped me up the mountain. Again, I was bent over and another student came by and said, "I hope you don't mind," as he took cotton or paper and wiped pus off the base of my spine. He then proceeded on up the hill.

I found this dream even more remarkable because, in waking life, I had conflicts with both of the students in the dream. Why not choose students to help me whom I felt kindly toward? As I considered my dream's choice of students, I realized that it was the students who caused the most conflict in me that could most encourage my spiritual growth.

From that night I never approached my students with the same mental attitude. Whenever I encountered a particularly antagonistic student and I began to respond negatively, I stopped myself, reminded myself that each student taught me, helped me on my spiritual path. But this mental attitude was only possible when my heart was open.

When I told Elizabeth Kent my dream, she said that *kundalini* energy at the base of the spine was thought to be like a snake unfolding as you gain enlightenment. Enlightenment occurs as *kundalini* moves up the spine to the top of the head. Perhaps the pus represented the popping of an infected blockage, a blockage which kept *kundalini* from unfolding and moving up the spine.

Oh, yes, during the height of this experience, there was searing pain just to the left side of my right breast. I felt as though my heart was being torn open.

Join Cardiac Rehabilitation Team

In the winter of 1989, I did a program on stress management at the local hospital. The next morning, when I arrived at my college office, I found a note on the door. It was from the Medical Director of the Cardiac Rehabilitation Program, which was located in the local hospital.

In the note, the Medical Director asked me to join his "team" as psychologist, and to consult with the cardiac program and its patients. This was volunteer work and I readily agreed, as it provided yet another opportunity for me to be of service to others.

I liked working with the cardiac patients because they were highly motivated to make changes in their lives. Many had undergone heart surgery, making them members of the "zipper club." They each bore a large scar running down their chests. When I met with the cardiac patients for the first time, I would encourage the men to expose their chests and reveal their scars. This display was always a very powerful moment in the group.

Their brush with death gave them the motivation to make serious lifestyle changes, and I was inspired by their will to live, their determination. Many of my college students thought they would live forever, so my work with cardiac patients was a stark contrast.

For eleven years I met with all Phase Two patients in the Cardiac Rehabilitation Program, and instructed them in stress management and relaxation skills. I never received any money for my services, and was always thankful that I had the opportunity to be of service to those in need.

Periodically, at the hospital I would do a program open to the community and charge a small amount. This money I spent on relaxation tapes, books, and biofeedback equipment for the Cardiac Rehabilitation Program.

Meet My Guru – Roy Eugene Davis

During Winter Quarter, a student in my Introduction to Counseling class did a presentation on meditation. When she mentioned that there was a meditation center in the next county, I was pleasantly surprised and immediately called the Center for Spiritual Awareness (CSA) in Lakemont, Georgia.

During my conversation, I learned that Roy Eugene Davis, a direct disciple of Paramahansa Yogananda, was the founder and head of the organization. Though Roy was traveling for several weeks and would not be in attendance, there was a meditation session every Sunday at 10:00 a.m. I attended the next Sunday.

Carolyn Davis officiated during the meditation. She read a short passage of Roy's teachings and we sat in the silence for some twenty-five minutes. Carolyn was such a sweet spirit and had a wonderful, soft voice. I immediately felt comfortable meditating with her and the few other people who appeared, and I decided to begin attending every Sunday.

I took comfort in the cross and picture of Jesus Christ above the altar. All the rest of the altar seemed quite foreign and exotic to me, but the cross and Jesus' picture were familiar and reassuring.

After a few weeks, Roy returned to CSA and began leading the Sunday meditations. Since moving to Panther Brook, I had been looking for a group of people who felt it was worthwhile to join together and sit in the silence. It was such a gift to my spiritual life to discover CSA, which was only eleven miles from my home.

I could not believe my good fortune in having Roy Eugene Davis available to me every week!

The following Information comes from the cover jacket, *Paramahansa Yogananda As I Knew Him*, by Roy Eugene Davis, CSA Press, Lakemont, Georgia, 2005. Used with Permission.

> Roy Eugene Davis has taught meditation and spiritual growth processes in North and South America, Europe, West Africa, and Japan, and India for more than 50 years. Some of his books have been published in 10 languages and 11 countries. He is the founder and spiritual director of Center for Spiritual Awareness.

> Paramahansa Yogananda (1893 – 1952) traveled from India to America in 1920 to teach the practical means by which people in all walks of life could nurture their spiritual growth and awaken to Self- and God-realization.

> He emphasized Kriya Yoga: intensive spiritual practices that unify (yoga) the practitioner's attention and awareness with infinite Consciousness. During his thirty-two years of ministry, he lectured to multitudes of people,

taught more than one hundred thousand of them advanced meditation methods, wrote many books, trained many disciples, and directed the activities of an organization that continues to spread his God-centered teachings throughout the world.

Roy Eugene Davis studied and practiced meditation under the personal guidance of Paramahansa Yogananda and was ordained by him in 1951.

When I first started going to CSA, I knew essentially nothing about Paramahansa Yogananda. After having spent many hours with Roy Eugene Davis and hearing him tell numerous stories about his "Master," I now feel great love and affection for Yogananda. His *Cosmic Chants* draw me to super-consciousness. Yogananda's classic, *Autobiography of a Yogi*, repeatedly inspires me. For more information, see www.yogananda-srf.org

Initiation into Kriya Yoga and Kriya Pranayama Meditation

From June 18 – 24, 1989, I attended a week-long, intensive yoga seminar with Roy Eugene Davis. During the seminar, Roy taught meditation and the art of balanced spiritual living. On Thursday he initiated me into Kriya Yoga, including Kriya Pranayama. Kriya Pranayama is a powerful meditation technique, which I immediately began practicing.

Roy taught the following:

Spiritual enlightenment provides accurate knowledge of our essence of being and of ultimate Reality and its varied processes. It is the result of soul- or Self-revelation. Effective Kriya Yoga practices remove conditions that interfere with Self-knowing and allow our consciousness to be restored to its original, pure wholeness.

I have been meditating/praying with Roy and participating in Center for Spiritual Awareness programs since we first met. Roy's teachings and writings are extremely clear and direct. He and his ministry have had a powerful influence on my spiritual life, and I have a great deal of love and respect for him. Roy can be contacted at www.csa-davis.org

In the Eye of the Hurricane – Dad's Transition

From July 19 – 22, 1990, I attended a retreat titled "In the Eye of the Hurricane" at Southern Dharma. The retreat was led by Dr. Susan Macdonald, who became a devotee of Sri Swami Satchidananda in 1970.

As part of the retreat, Susan provided time for creative writing. I chose to write *Dad's Transition*. I would write; I would cry; I would write; I would cry. The wounds were deep and raw. Near the end of the retreat, I read it aloud to the group. I also gave permission to publish it in the SDRC Newsletter, and I included it in our yearly letter to friends. Writing *Dad's Transition* was extremely difficult but I felt it did further the healing process.

Dad's Transition
January 24, 1990

"Our father is in the final stages of dying." – my brother's voice came over the answering machine, the content of his message shocking, horrifying, repulsive... .

The previous couple of weeks had been spent trying to cope with a herniated disc in my lower spine. That day, so that I could teach my classes, my wife had driven me to school while I lay in the back seat of the car.

I knew Dad was dying from lung cancer and felt that on some level grief had broken my back. But death's speed caught me by surprise. I wondered if I could live without him, and had fantasies that I would die with him.

I spent that evening and much of the next day lying beside Dad in his bedroom, he in a hospital bed and I in a single bed. He could not speak but our eyes met many times. He was very agitated, breathing was labored, and he experienced much apnea, long periods between breaths. His weight loss, combined with his cancer, had forced his heart to the surface center of his chest. Each heartbeat was clearly visible.

I felt deeply the distress of his agitated, clinging mind. On that second evening I sat by his bed, put my hand on his body, and began a mindfulness of breath meditation. I joined with him in his breathing, matching my breath to his, counting ten breaths and then beginning anew.

I rejoiced as his agitation ceased and his breathing became less labored. In the last moments of his seventy-five years of this existence, Dad and I meditated together, something we had never done.

After about twenty minutes, our meditation session ended and I went to take a shower. As I cleansed myself, I was in awe of this process we all must face – this process of dying. And I was reminded of the purification ceremony just before the birth of my son. That also involved cleansing and, in addition, wearing hospital garments. Was not Dad's death a birth? Was not his a transition to another existence?

Thus purified, I rejoined him and began his induction to death. I once again matched my breathing with his and began counting breaths, and once again his agitation diminished. Then I and the two others in the room read prayers and sang songs. One or two tears rolled down Dad's cheek and he raised his hand as if waving "Goodbye."

Finally I began our last mindfulness of breath meditation, matching my breathing to Dad's. But the periods between breaths became so very long that I knew I would have to choose whether to go with Dad or to stay – death or life. I had the freedom to make a conscious choice; Dad did not. I chose life and sat by him as he made his transition – eyes open but not seeing.

For much of the time prior to his funeral I stayed with Dad's body. I rested on the floor by his coffin and sat in a chair touching him as I read prayers and meditated. My practice consisted mostly of Kriya Yoga, Heart, and Forgiveness meditations. That vigil by Dad's body helped heal much of the pain that existed between us, and I am forever thankful to him for allowing me to assist during his transition.

A New Year's Retreat

I attended a New Year's Retreat at Southern Dharma from December 28, 1990 to January 5, 1991. The retreat was led by John Orr and Marcia Rose. Like John, Marcia was an Insight Meditation teacher.

The morning of the first day, I was sitting in the swivel chair by the fire and began to have a real anxiety attack. I really thought I was about to throw up my breakfast into my bowl of cereal.

I did not want to stay and face my demons, my pain. I went to John later and asked if I needed to tell him if I decided to leave. He asked me to let him know. That afternoon I began my daily walks up the mountain – forty-five minutes to the junction in the road, and later an hour to the top.

When I returned that first day from my hike, I cried, sobbed intensely – crying out against the pain! Intense crying lasted about twenty minutes and I felt my heart open – layers of armor, protection from Dad's death, and pain of daily life lifting. I cried several times during the retreat, but never so intensely again – opening my heart to Life!!!

During the retreat my back hurt so much that I was forced to meditate lying down. I was having trouble focusing and staying awake. Jeff Collins, who had just finished a three month retreat at Insight Meditation Society in Barre, MA, suggested that I use my body's contact points as focus points for meditation. He had learned this technique at I.M.S.

I used the heels of my feet, the buttocks, and the back of my head. On the in-breath I would note the contact, and, as I became more focused, feel the energy flow from my heels, up my legs, joining the spine, and moving up the spinal pathway to the head. On the out-breath I could feel the energy moving down the front of my body and down my legs to my feet.

I found I could meditate like this for the entire forty-five to sixty minutes, and my body seemed to be more charged with energy. I was really cooking in that corner of the meditation hall!

I sat up for one, one-hour sitting as John did a meditation focused on the chakras. I could feel each chakra quite clearly, except for the sternum, which is associated with power – something I have trouble accepting and using. I had trouble with colors – visualizing them – but could note brightness of light.

When John suggested pure white light pouring through my body from the crown chakra, I was bathed in this light and had no pain anywhere in my body. I lay there for what seemed like a long time, maybe twenty minutes, not able to feel my body but only perceiving myself as pure spirit. A marvelous experience!!!

The Inner Sound A couple of days later I was continuing my meditation focused on my three contact points and I began to hear the inner sound. I had heard it briefly twice previously during the retreat, each time following my hike up the mountain and a shower.

But this time it became so loud I could not hear anything else in the meditation hall. It was a loud rushing sound. It continued for the whole meditation and subsided as John began chanting.

The only other time I had heard this inner sound was on a Sunday at CSA, when I was thinking about quitting my job and going to my parent's home to care for Dad until he died. I was in such anguish, such indecisiveness, that the sound was very comforting. The sound visited as if a friend.

Marcia Rose said the sound was the "sound of silence." It was always there within us if we became still and quiet. At CSA, I was encouraged to listen to the sound and follow it to its source. It was considered a deeper, more effective meditation technique than watching the inner light.

During my eight days of silence, I continued to work on my grief caused by my father's transition. I relived his death – flashbacks occurred when I felt my son's heart beat or when a tear rolled down my cheek. Death was so normal and yet I had been so insulated from it.

At the end of January, I returned to my parent's home to engage in a ceremony marking the end of a year of grieving for Dad. I hoped this ceremony would help me move on in my life. I hoped this action would also help my mother move on with her life.

Himalayan Institute

During October 23 – 27, 1991, I attended a Counselors and Therapists Training Seminar at the Himalayan Institute in Honesdale, Pennsylvania. The program had a strong biofeedback component, and that was an area of inquiry I wanted to pursue.

Marty Wuttke, a fellow meditator at CSA, attended the program a year earlier and highly recommended it. Roy Eugene Davis had ordained Marty as a CSA minister and Marty regularly attended the Sunday morning meditations. Marty also presented afternoon workshops on biofeedback during the week-long retreats at CSA.

Marty worked at an addiction treatment center, where he did biofeedback training with the clients. He was very interested in biofeedback and freely shared his knowledge with me. A couple of times Marty placed electrodes on my head and did some brain wave biofeedback.

As a result of attending Marty's workshops and experiencing brain wave biofeedback, I learned to identify my brain waves. I found the ability to understand and identify my brain waves helpful. If you are interested in brain wave biofeedback, check out Marty's website www.neurotherapy.us

Roy Eugene Davis thought Swami Rama's work was solid and spoke highly of him and the Himalayan Institute, which Swami Rama had founded. The devotees at Himalayan Institute dedicated themselves to using Western-based scientific principles to prove the effectiveness of Eastern-based yoga and meditative therapies.

They presented a holistic and integrated program which examined the roles of physiological interventions (diet, exercise, relaxation, biofeedback, and hatha yoga). Based on the recommendations of Roy Eugene Davis and Marty Wuttke, I decided to attend the seminar.

After I settled in my room at the Himalayan Institute, I walked outside and saw Swami Rama playing tennis. He played alone on his side of the court while several players were on the other side. Some people were standing around watching and talking. As I approached the tennis court, Swami Rama turned to me, tennis racket in one hand and tennis ball in the other, and peered deeply into my soul.

I immediately felt his presence trying to invade my heart, and I stopped dead in my tracks and just stood there. It was as if I could not move! But I was not ready to open my heart to him, and silently told him so, at which point he turned back to the other players and served the ball.

This experience was unlike any other, and I had difficulty deciding if it was real or just imagined. I wanted to know more about Swami Rama before I opened my heart to his powerful influence.

While it is obvious to me that Swami Rama accomplished many great things, I do not regret that I did not open my heart to him. When I remember this encounter with Swami Rama, I often think gratefully of my encounter with another Swami, Swami Satchidananda. Six years later Swami Satchidananda also attempted to come into my heart, and this time I welcomed this transfer of *kundalini shakti* with an open heart. I knew enough about Swami Satchidananda, the founder of Integral Yoga®, to trust that his efforts would be for my highest good.

The Counselors and Therapists Training Seminar at the Himalayan Institute was an excellent, systematic introduction to the techniques and underlying principles of yoga and meditative therapy. My participation at Southern Dharma and the Center for Spiritual Awareness had already introduced me to many of the concepts, but the Himalayan Institute staff presented the material as a unified whole.

Their emphasis on nasal wash, nasal dominance, diaphragmatic breathing, alternate nostril breathing, and biofeedback enhanced my personal practice and my work with my students, cardiac patients, and others. For more information on their programs, see www.himalayaninstitute.org

Thermal Biofeedback Biofeedback as a means to discover internal processes has really fascinated and intrigued me. The concept that there is a direct link between finger temperature and cortical activity is particularly useful.

You probably already have a thermometer sitting around your home somewhere. If you do, go find it. If you do not, go buy one. It can be quite inexpensive and will provide you useful information about how stressed you are and the effectiveness of your relaxation strategies.

Hold the tip of your thermometer (thermistor) with your thumb and index finger. You may instead wish to tape the thermistor to the index finger. If you do use tape, be sure not to wrap the tape all the way around your finger, as that would restrict blood flow to the finger. Just use enough tape to attach the thermistor.

Once you know your finger temperature, try to increase it by increasing the blood flow to your hand. Use the relaxation skills you already have or try some you are learning in this book. Generally, as finger temperature increases, alpha and theta brain wave activity, which is associated with relaxation, also increases.

Finger Temperature
70°-80° = high stress
80°-85° = moderate stress
85°-90° = stressed
90°-95° = good
95°- up = excellent

With some exceptions, finger temperature is a good judge of a person's stress level. My Phase Two cardiac patients often had finger temperature in the low 70's. They were usually chronic chest breathers, denying their bodies sufficient oxygen. When they learned to raise their finger temperature to the low 80's, they reported being more relaxed than they had ever been. Without thermal biofeedback, they would never know how much more they could achieve.

The clinical goal is a finger temperature of 95 degrees. (It is more difficult to move finger temperature from the 80's to the 90's than from the 70's to the 80's.)

That is the joy of biofeedback! It tells us what is actually happening in our bodies. I once worked with a student who insisted he was not stressed; he just had circulation problems, which caused cold hands. One day he fell asleep in class. I quietly walked over to him and touched his hands. They were extremely warm. When I woke him, his hands immediately got cold. This little experiment convinced me that he was, indeed, chronically stressed.

Please keep in mind that, from a meditation/prayer standpoint, being totally relaxed is very helpful. Remember that the definition of meditation is "a relaxed, focused, uninterrupted awareness." The ability to relax, to let go, is key to success in meditation.

Of course, there are some confounding variables that must be considered when using thermal biofeedback. If the room is too cold or too hot, finger temperature may not be valid. Some people are "thermal responders," that is, their fingers are always warm, no matter how stressed they are. Other people have circulation problems and their hands are always cold. For these reasons I also recommend that you use a GSR (Electrodermal) biofeedback device. It will not have thermal biofeedback's confounding variables.

Electrodermal Biofeedback Electrodermal biofeedback [aka skin conductance or galvanic skin response (GSR) biofeedback] is more difficult to manipulate than thermal biofeedback. Because it is so difficult to manipulate and artificially control, it is one of the modalities utilized in a lie detector test.

Since electrodermal biofeedback is more difficult, it is often used after one has achieved mastery of thermal biofeedback. Raising your finger temperature is easier than increasing the electrical conductance of your skin.

Around twenty years ago I purchased thirty-five GSR2 units from Thought Technology and, during the following years, used them with a variety of populations – pre-school, middle and high school, college students, cardiac patients, alcohol and drug addicts, participants in relaxation and stress management workshops, and individual clients. Once, I carried the device for an entire day and learned much about what caused me stress and what relaxed me.

> The GSR2 precisely monitors your stress levels by translating tiny tension-related changes in skin pores into a rising or falling tone. By resting two fingers on the sensing plates you learn to lower the pitch and your stress level. You basically get "biological" feedback through the GSR2 as you learn to relax and as you get better at doing it, you'll find yourself relaxing faster with or without the GSR2. (Quoted from www.thoughttechnology.com Used with permission)

If you do not already have access to a GSR device, I recommend you purchase Thought Technology's "GSR2 Biofeedback Relaxation System." It holds up well and is a useful learning tool. The current price is around $75.00 and includes the biofeedback unit, earphone, instructional CD (side 1: "How to get the most from your GSR2," side 2: "fully-narrated relaxation exercise"), 9V battery and operator's manual. If you mention this book, *Spiritual Autobiography and Meditation Handbook,* you will receive a 10% discount. To order, go to www.thoughttechnology.com

The Crocodile Posture As infants, one hundred percent of us start out life as diaphragmatic breathers. Unfortunately, as we age, eighty percent of us shift to chest breathing. Chest breathing is very inefficient breathing, chronically depriving us of the vital oxygen we need for good health.

This shallow breathing creates a chronic stress response, increasing our blood pressure, heart rate, muscle tension, etc. It also decreases alpha and theta brain wave activity – brain waves associated with relaxation. This chronic stress response also increases the likelihood of developing addictions.

Regrettably, many of us no longer know how to use the muscles needed for diaphragmatic breathing. The Himalayan Institute staff emphasized the usefulness of the Crocodile Posture in teaching the correct muscles to use in breathing.

The Crocodile Posture is accomplished by lying on the stomach, legs about hip-width apart and toes pointing in or out, folding arms and placing hands on the opposite elbows, drawing elbows in toward body so that the shoulders and upper chest are off the floor, resting forehead on arms, closing eyes and relaxing. This posture locks the chest muscles so the person is forced to breathe diaphragmatically, thus teaching the correct muscles to use while breathing.

The Himalayan Institute staff also recommended using a sandbag to help strengthen the muscles used in diaphragmatic breathing. The instructions were to lie on the back, place the bag over the lower belly, and practice making the bag rise on the in-breath. While in Pennsylvania, I purchased a sandbag, but I must confess I have not often used it, either personally or with my students.

Neti (Nasal) Wash My second visit to the Himalayan Institute occurred from June 4 –10, 1992. While there I attended a seminar on "Strengthening the Immune System" and participated in training in biofeedback and relaxation techniques. During my visit, I had an opportunity to discuss with John Clarke, M.D., the Medical Director, my difficulty in doing a neti wash (nasal wash).

A neti wash involves pouring warm saline solution through one nostril and then the other. Years earlier I had tried doing a daily neti wash because Roy Eugene Davis recommended it. Almost immediately, I got an ear ache. I had always had a problem with ear aches and I feared a nasal wash would lead to them.

Dr. Clarke drew a picture of the human head on the board and insisted that, even if I held my head upright, I could pour water into one nostril and it would come out the other without entering the ear canal.

With this encouragement, I returned home and began a daily nasal wash. I found that Dr. Clarke was correct and I encountered no problems. I have continued to do nasal washes daily or twice daily, and am sure my health has improved because of it.

In yoga, breathing freely through both nostrils is said to aid in harmonizing the active and passive systems of the body, and therefore the neti wash is a helpful practice before meditation. Alternate nostril breathing, a powerful pranayama, is very difficult to do well if the nose is congested.

Neti wash (nasal wash) containers can be easily purchased in most nationwide chain stores, near the pharmacy area. They are not expensive. If you can buy a porcelain neti pot, it can be easily cleaned and can last a long time. If you buy a large container of salt, make sure it contains no additives, especially iodine.

Reverend Bo Turner

In early 1992, I was looking over the local county newspaper and read an article written by a Baptist minister named Bo Turner. I had seen other articles and letters written by him that I enjoyed reading. In this article, Bo described his church in Tallulah Falls and invited anyone interested to attend.

I liked what he was writing in his articles and decided to stop by Bo's church after the Sunday morning meditation at CSA. As I heard Bo preach, I was attracted to both his message and ministry.

Bo ministered to men at a nearby Christian treatment center. Men with few resources who were addicted to alcohol or drugs – but motivated to change – were offered a free, twelve-week, residential program at the center. The men attended Bo's church almost every Sunday and Bo often tailored his message to their needs.

Because his socially engaged form of Christianity lacked mass appeal in this rural, fundamentalist Christian, Southern Appalachian area, Bo's church was extremely small. My Sunday routine gradually became going to CSA for meditation and then stopping by Tallulah Falls Baptist Church for services before heading home. In time, I began leading the singing for the church – another opportunity for service.

Eventually Bo asked me to join the Board of Trustees of the Christian residential treatment center for addicted men, and I was pleased to do so. It provided yet another opportunity to be of service to others. I worked with the men and served on the Board of Trustees for ten years.

Follower of Christ My many hours with Bo helped me rediscover my identity as a Christian, to be more comfortable with my Christian heritage and Christian beliefs. Bo was a "follower of Christ" and his example inspired me to also strive to be a "follower of Christ." Though I still did not call myself a "Christian" – I had met too many of those who were not true followers of Christ.

I am reminded of what Mahatma Gandhi once said. The teachings of Jesus Christ were so powerful that he was tempted to become a Christian. However, meeting Christians and seeing how they failed to live Christ's teachings turned him off the idea.

Bo's Transition On July 15, 2005, the Reverend Bo Turner made his transition. Brother Bo died quite unexpectedly. I visited the funeral home and said prayers over his body. Death continues to be such a mystery to me. *Dukkha, Annica, Annatta* – suffering, death, impermanence, no-self – all were <u>such</u> mysteries to me!

Bo was such a <u>strong</u>, powerful personality and it was hard to believe he was gone. Bo's ministry focused on trying to expand folk's spiritual understanding and practices by stretching their limits and reminding them what Christ actually said and did. He cared deeply for others and wanted them to behave better, to lead Christ-like lives. I was thankful to know him and call him my friend.

God is Without Form and Name While finding deep, personal satisfaction as a follower of Christ, I recognize that God, as the enlivening power of the universe, is without form and without name. I understand the wisdom of Integral Yoga's® motto, "Truth is One - Paths are Many." Therefore all spiritual paths are honored at Panther Brook Spiritual Center.

Sri Swami Satchidananda, the founder of Integral Yoga®, expressed this well when talking of the finite and the infinite:

> If you go deeper into the philosophy and scriptures of all the religions, you'll find out that they all say there's only one God and that God is omnipresent, omnipotent, omniscient. If God is everywhere, how can God have one form and one name? All these forms and names are God. In the real sense, God is formless, nameless, abstract, the Absolute One. You can call it Absolute Consciousness, Cosmic Consciousness, Cosmic Intelligence or the Cosmic Force; or, according to the scientists, you can call it basic matter and force, the essence or the thing in itself. It's impossible for our limited minds to grasp the Unlimited One. So, the finite mind takes a little part of that infinite that it can understand and says, "That's God for me." (Used with Permission)

First Yoga Class

In September I participated in my local hospital's L.I.F.E. program by teaching relaxation skills during a four-week class entitled "In the Eye of Life's Hurricane." The class cost $30.00 or $20.00 if students registered for the yoga class which preceded it.

The yoga class was taught by Manjula Spears, an Integral Yoga® certified instructor. In 1990, Manjula had come to the hospital and taught a yoga class which I had taken. It was my first yoga class and I began to practice at home. My yoga practice immediately deepened my meditation practice, so I instantly became a fan.

Manjula has devoted her life to yoga. She has taken several training courses and taught for many years. She is an excellent teacher! For more information about her programs, see http://www.satchidanandamission.com Manjula may be contacted at satchidanandamission@gmail.com

The money I made from teaching the class was donated to the hospital's cardiac and pulmonary program so that relaxation tapes and biofeedback equipment could be purchased. In addition, I continued my ongoing commitment to serve as consultant to the cardiac program.

Among the handouts to my workshop participants were two pages written by Marty Wuttke. He gave these handouts to the addicts in his treatment center. These handouts reflected the emphasis on breath which was so important in yoga. They were simple but powerful intervention tools:

Diaphragmatic Breathing Exercise
By A. Martin Wuttke
(Used with Permission)

PURPOSE & BENEFITS:

The purpose of this exercise is to make you very conscious of your breathing patterns. By consciously regulating your breathing pattern and breathing in a manner that reflects deep relaxation, you interrupt the cycle of stress and, at the same time, release accumulated stress and tension from your mind and body.

WHEN TO PRACTICE:

Four times a day, 5-10 minutes each practice session.
Ideally:
1. Before getting out of bed in AM.
2. Before lunch.
3. Before dinner.
4. After you are in bed, before you go to sleep.

HOW TO PRACTICE:

1. Get as comfortable as possible – relax your muscles.

2. Take three complete, deep, cleansing breaths.

3. Breathe diaphragmatically: Concentrate on your abdomen – between your navel and the lower part of your sternum. (Place your hand there if you are having difficulty.)

4. Breathe only moving your abdomen: As you inhale your abdomen should expand and rise slightly; as you exhale your abdomen should contract. Keep your shoulders and the rest of your body completely still.

5. (a) For general relaxation: Make the length of inhalation the same as the length of exhalation. (If you inhale to the count of three, exhale to the count of three.)

5. (b) For insomnia, hyper arousal and panic symptoms (NOT FOR DEPRESSION): Make your exhalation twice the length of your inhalation. (If you inhale to the count of three, exhale to the count of six.)

6. Breathe only through your nose – make your breath smooth, rhythmic, gentle, silent – with as little effort as possible.

7. If thoughts intrude, just keep returning your attention back to your breath.

8. Continue for 5-10 minutes.

Experience has taught me that, if you can learn to breathe diaphragmatically, it will solve many anxiety issues. During my career, several students have cited diaphragmatic breathing, belly breathing, as the **most important skill they have learned!!!** Many report having gained hours of additional sleep. They wake up in the middle of the night and, instead of staying awake, they focus on slow belly breathing and soon fall back asleep.

During the day, if they become anxious, they focus on slow belly breathing and the anxiety diminishes. In fact, research has shown that it is impossible to have an anxiety attack while belly breathing. To have an anxiety attack, you must be chest breathing. Rapid chest breathing can actually <u>cause</u> an anxiety attack! Therefore, if you want to stop an anxiety attack, move your breathing from the chest to the diaphragm, to your belly.

Alternate Nostril Breathing
By A. Martin Wuttke
(Used with Permission)

PURPOSE & BENEFITS:

The following technique produces a state of sympathetic/parasympathetic balance. It will also cause brainwave patterns to become more synchronized. The result will be a more settled, calm and centered state of being.

WHEN TO PRACTICE:

Alternate nostril breathing can either be performed by itself or as a preparation for any other type of relaxation exercise. (It is most beneficial before meditation.)

HOW TO PRACTICE:

1. Sit up straight... feet flat on the floor... spine, neck and head in alignment. Let your left hand rest on your left thigh, palm facing up... eyes closed.

2. Bring your right hand up so that your palm is in front of your face. You will be using your thumb to close the right nostril and your ring finger and little finger together to close the left nostril. Curl your index and middle finger into the palm of your hand and just let them relax.

3. Take a deep inhalation ... close the right nostril with your thumb and exhale through the left nostril ... inhale through the left nostril ... close left nostril with your ring and little finger ... release thumb and exhale through right nostril ... inhale through right nostril ... (That completes one cycle.) ... close right nostril with your thumb . . . release ring and little finger and exhale through left nostril.

EXAMPLE:
Exhale left
Inhale left

Exhale right
Inhale right
makes one full cycle
Exhale left

4. Your breath should flow quietly in a smooth even rhythm without any pauses, breaks or jerkiness. Your inhalation and exhalation should be even in length.

5. Begin with five full cycles of alternate nostril breathing. When the exercise becomes effortless and smooth, you can go as high as twelve cycles.

Alternate nostril breathing is a useful prelude to your meditation/prayer time. By balancing the two hemispheres of the brain, prefect conditions are created for deep meditations. When you have mastered the technique, begin to make the exhalations longer than the inhalations, eventually twice as long.

But remember to **never strain** while doing any of the breathing exercises. If you find yourself gasping for air, back off immediately! Just relax and breathe normally. With practice, you will eventually develop better breath control and experience its benefits.

Professional Biofeedback Training

Held in Philadelphia, Pennsylvania, the Professional Biofeedback Certificate Program ran from July 10 – 18, 1993, and entailed an intense eighty hours of training. When I completed the training, I was much more comfortable working with the different biofeedback modalities, and felt I had a better understanding of them.

At one point during the biofeedback training, two women and I were working as a team with electrodermal and other biofeedback modalities. When my turn came to be the "subject",

I was hooked to the biofeedback machine and then I placed my left hand in a bucket filled with ice cubes and water. The "normal" reaction to such an event would be great stress, as most people would find immersion in ice water <u>very</u> painful.

But from my yoga training and meditation practice, I had learned to be a "witness" to the pain, and to interpret the pain as energy. I imagined the energy moving up my hand, through my arm, to the crown chakra at the top of my head. The energy thus served to elevate my consciousness!

Instead of reacting negatively, the biofeedback equipment indicated no change. The instructor came over to our group and indicated that this was a <u>very</u> unusual response to immersion in ice water! He added that it would be a useful coping mechanism whenever I actually experienced painful stimuli.

Introduction to Autogenic Training

For several years, I had discussed autogenic training in my Stress Management course. During each course, I spent part of a class period leading my students in an autogenic training exercise.

However, my training in Philadelphia gave me a new depth of understanding. The workshop leader included a lengthy discussion of the history and forms of autogenic training, and led us through an autogenic training exercise.

The autogenic training exercise was very helpful. While I lay on the floor to practice my instructor's directions, my mind went completely blank and I did not return to consciousness until the exercise ended. I was very impressed!

Over the years I have learned to appreciate the power of autogenic training. Having introduced hundreds of students to autogenics, I never cease to be amazed at some of their responses. Autogenic-induced states sometimes allow deeply repressed memories to surface in a most vivid, intense fashion.

During autogenic training, several of my students have had flashbacks to prior experiences of sexual and physical abuse. These remembrances were <u>so</u> vivid that, in some cases, students felt overwhelmed by them. Supportive therapy was required to assist them in learning to understand and deal with these memories.

I believe that <u>any</u> relaxation exercise can potentially produce these flashbacks. However, my experiences indicate that autogenic training, as a form of self-hypnosis, is a more powerful technique than most of the others.

It should, therefore, be approached with some care. Although particularly unpleasant "autogenic discharges" must be managed with clinical skill and sophistication, they are not to be avoided. Indeed, they indicate the power and usefulness of autogenic training.

Autogenic Training Instructions

Autogenic training is probably the world's most widely used self-regulation therapy. The term "autogenic" is derived from the Greek words *autos*, meaning self, and *genos*, meaning origin. Therefore, in this structured self-hypnosis technique, the self-regulation and self-healing powers of the mind are channeled in a positive manner, repeating phrases in a state of passive concentration.

Sit or lie in a physically relaxing position, allowing all thoughts and distractions to pass without judgments. Watch thoughts passively, as if you had entered a movie theatre and your thoughts were being shown on a movie screen in front of you, or you were riding in a car and your thoughts were like billboards passing on the highway.

While you concentrate on body sensations in a passive manner, without directly or volitionally bringing about any change, mentally repeat the following six phrases:

1. My (choose dominant arm) is very heavy. (Repeat four to six times.)
2. My (choose dominant arm) is very warm. (Repeat four to six times.)
3. My heartbeat is calm and regular. (Repeat four to six times.)
4. It breathes me. (Repeat four to six times.)
5. My solar plexus is warm. (Repeat four to six times.)
6. My forehead is cool. (Repeat four to six times.)

Periodically, while repeating the six standard phrases, you should occasionally repeat one or more of the following positive intentions:

I am calm.
I am relaxed.
I am quiet.

If deep relaxation is not achieved immediately, you may rest assured that it will come later, with more practice.

When you successfully achieve an autogenic state, it should not be abruptly terminated. Rather, you should slowly reactivate muscular and breathing systems. This is achieved by wiggling the fingers and toes, breathing in deeply a few times, and, finally, opening the eyes.

Please note that blood vessel dilation and associative relaxation have a particularly tranquilizing and sleep inducing effect. However, blood vessel dilation is not harmless, since the changed distribution of blood influences the entire organism. Therefore, autogenic training should only be instituted by healthy individuals for whom no vascular risks are known to exist.

Twenty-four Hour Retreats at Panther Brook Spiritual Center

Beginning August 13, 1993, I began periodically spending twenty-four hours in silence, solitude, meditation and prayer. These short retreats helped me maintain my peace within, helped me maintain balance and concentration.

Panther Brook Spiritual Center was wonderful space for these retreats. The Center was the first thing I built when we bought the property in 1987. It was built for love of God, and had only been used for spiritual practice. I set the windows lower than normal so I could see out while sitting on the floor. It never occurred to me back then that someday I would be meditating in a chair.

While on retreat in Panther Brook Spiritual Center, I was away from the main house, but still on the property. I turned off the phone and my family knew that I was not to be disturbed unless fire or blood was involved. Through the years, I have spent many wonderful hours there in super-consciousness, bliss-consciousness.

1993 Thanksgiving Freedom from Addiction Celebration

When we moved to Panther Brook in 1987, I was no longer smoking dope. My daily meditation practice made getting high on drugs superfluous. I got <u>so</u> blissed out in God-consciousness that the experience made my addiction unnecessary. So I buried my "stash" of marijuana and hashish in my dirt basement.

My work as a volunteer at a Christian treatment center for men with drug and alcohol addictions continued to help me in my own spiritual growth. With my own personal experiences in mind, I designed and implemented a daily relaxation therapy program.

The men listened to tapes designed to help them learn and practice relaxation skills. I also met with them weekly. Using biofeedback equipment, I had them practice a variety of relaxation techniques, including diaphragmatic breathing, alternate nostril breathing, progressive muscle relaxation, and meditation/prayer.

During one of our weekly sessions, one man announced, "I'm not an addict. I just like having a bottle of bourbon in the back of my closet." As I verbally debunked his mythology, I thought to myself, "What a hypocrite you are, Dr. Brooking! You say you are no longer addicted to marijuana but you keep a large stash in your basement. You never completely let it go."

I resolved to end my hypocrisy and destroy my stash. How could I really have faith in God as long as I kept my safety net, my stash around?

Unfortunately, my back was really giving me problems, so I actually had to hire a man to dig up my stash in the basement. Complicating things even further was the fact that I had built a large wood pile on top of the stash and had forgotten exactly where the stash was buried.

So my paid worker had to take all the wood out of the basement, and then, using a metal rod, poke into the dirt until he located the stash. He then dug it up and gave it to me. After covering the hole, he then replaced all the wood. I never did tell him what was in the bundle he dug up. I did not think it would be a good idea.

I started a fire and burned up all the drug paraphernalia. The actual marijuana and hashish I took down to Panther Brook. Over the years, when I encountered a particularly good, powerful smoke, I would save a little bit "for the future." These had accumulated until my many small packs added up to quite a large stash. I opened each packet and carefully emptied its contents into the stream.

I experienced such interesting feelings as I witnessed it all float down stream! Thanksgiving was a perfect time for this ceremony, as I was so thankful to be free of that addiction!!!

I also had jars of marijuana seeds which I dumped into Panther Brook. As the seeds floated downstream, I envisioned the whole watershed being littered with marijuana plants the next summer; but I never did find any.

To top off this Thanksgiving Freedom from Addiction Celebration, I took a gallon of "white lightning" and poured it on the ground. It had been given to me many years earlier while living in the western North Carolina Mountains, and I rejoiced that, through my meditation/prayer practice, my desire for alcohol had also vanished!

Addictions are Spiritual Diseases This Thanksgiving celebration was only made possible by my meditation practice and God's grace. At their core, I am convinced that addictions are spiritual diseases. To be complete, my spiritual autobiography must include my addictions, and, by God's grace, how they evaporated.

During the 1960's, Timothy Leary extolled the power of drugs for spiritual growth. I, and many others, enthusiastically followed his directives: "Turn On – Tune In – Drop Out!" Well, I never totally dropped out, but I certainly embraced turning on and tuning in.

1969 – Acid and Woodstock From my campsite at the 1969 Woodstock festival, I could see a pond, where I spent several hours enjoying the water and camaraderie. From the Woodstock pond I could faintly hear the music. It was muffled but filled the air. The first day of the festival was devoted primarily to folk music, of which I was particularly fond. Eventually, I left the pond, stopped by my camp for some food, and wandered toward the music.

Between musical acts, announcements were made, many about folks separated and lost, some asking that people get down from the speaker/light towers because they might collapse from the weight. Regular announcements were also made about bad acid, especially bad brown. Other announcements explained that the brown acid was not poisoned; it was just made badly.

I wanted to visit the bad trip tent, especially given my own bad trip earlier in the summer. The tent itself was quite large, containing several cots and full of people. I could not believe what I saw there – people screaming, crying, and vomiting. It was like a trip to hell, and yet only a few minutes walk from the peaceful, joyous pond with all of its loving people.

I felt great empathy and sympathy for those tormented souls in the bad trip tent. Seeing their pain brought back memories of my own experiences just a few months earlier.

First Acid Trip On May 8, 1969, I took my first acid trip. I had a summer job in Miami and decided to sublet my Philadelphia apartment for the summer. I chose a hippie drug dealer to take care of my apartment, which contained all of my worldly goods. He gave me a hit of acid to seal the deal.

As the acid slowly came on, I walked down to the Philadelphia Art Museum and Fairmont Park. It was a beautiful, warm day in May and the sun felt quite wonderful. In time I met a good looking Hispanic girl who was about my age. At this point the acid was peaking nicely and I was intrigued because I was having quite an unusual reaction to her.

She was a being of pure light, a part of Divine Consciousness, just as I, also, was a spark of pure, divine, consciousness. For the first time in my life, *__I lost all prejudices__*! All stereotypes dissolved into the acid. As a true "Son of the South," I had been thoroughly steeped in prejudices and stereotypes, and suddenly a new, radical level of consciousness emerged. I felt so liberated, so free!!!

Only the present moment dominated my consciousness. As we talked of many things, I experienced pure listening for the first time in my life. There was no judgment as I listened, no thought as to how I should respond – only pure, simple listening. Our time together was such <u>JOY</u>!

I am convinced that my first acid trip did allow me to glimpse a higher level of consciousness, and this glimpse proved to be life changing. The next time I saw my hippie drug dealer, I gave him one hundred dollars and asked him for as many hits of acid as the money would buy. Unfortunately, the acid he sold me was not as pure as that first hit.

Third Acid Trip On June 15, 1969, in Miami, Florida, I took my third acid trip. This trip almost destroyed me, and left me psychologically quite shattered. It began innocently enough when I met this guy and he came to my apartment so we could drop some acid together. My roommate was gone and we had the place to ourselves. We smoked a lot of dope and hashish, dropped the acid, and waited for what seemed like a long time, but nothing happened.

My friend said he had some mescaline and, since the acid was a bust, why not take the mescaline. I thought that was a great idea, so we did. Now a trip on acid can be a subtle journey, and we were well along the journey when we did the mescaline. We just did not know it. Unfortunately, we discovered our misperceptions too late to correct them.

I distinctly remember my friend yelling, "Be my kite man! GOD, OH GOD, BE MY KITE MAN!!!" He was weeping, huddled in a fetal position in a corner of the room.

My vision was completely distorted, and it seemed like I could see only strands of light, wave particles revealing nothing solid – emptiness permeating everything.   As the mescaline hit, everything speeded up.   I began to vibrate intensely; wave particles flowed quickly.   I began to disintegrate, not only "I" psychologically, but also "I" physically. How could I be my friend's kite man? There was no ground; there was no "me." I, too, found myself on the floor, in a fetal position....

I am not sure how long we tripped like this, each of us in a fetal position on the floor. It felt like lifetimes, though I suspect only a few hours. This was by no means a pleasant experience. Rather terrifying in nature and duration, this ordeal showed no signs of abating. Finally, through clinched teeth, I suggested to my friend that we take some Thorazine. My friend immediately agreed.

Now the problem for me was how to pull my fractured self together sufficiently to get up, open the drawer, find and open the bottle, and swallow the pill.   I remember, when the drawer opened, the entire contents fell all over the room. Of course, like everything else, the room was not solid and so finding the bottle in all that empty space was <u>exceedingly</u> difficult! Opening it and swallowing were not easy either!!!

Eventually, we took the Thorazine; and its effect felt like a heavy, wool blanket descending upon me. As the hallucinations and delusions slowly diminished, we decided to escape the apartment and take a drive. I do not know how long we drove or where we went, but we stopped at this small bridge and I walked down to the water below.

I sat on a rock, just trying to pull myself together. It was now daylight and I suddenly became aware of movement all around me. Everything was alive and sought to live – the flowers actually opened to the sun's rays, as did the insects, the shells, the animals, everything. The salt water and tide pools were full of life – I could see nothing but life living on life. I looked at my arms and my hands and realized that I, too, was a part of this cycle. I began to weep, tears of joy, tears of understanding....

A Week of Acid Since my first, consciousness-expanding, wonderful acid trip, I had not been able to equal the experience, though I had dropped acid a number of times. I decided I was not dropping enough acid to break through my resistance to opening up, expanding my consciousness. So on February 12, 1970, I resolved to take acid every day for a week. More frequent, more intense trips would be better, I hypothesized.

Unfortunately, my week-long acid trip just made me psychotic as hell. I got so paranoid that, at the end of the week, I called a friend and asked if I could bring my stash of drugs over to him. When he agreed to keep it for me, I drove it over to his place. During the entire trip I was certain a telephone truck full of police was following me.

The interesting thing about paranoia is that there is always the possibility it is <u>not</u> paranoia, that there actually <u>WAS</u> a telephone truck following me. After all, every time I looked around, there <u>was</u> a telephone truck within sight.

Anyway, my friend kept the drugs for me until I got a little less crazy, and then returned them. He shared with me that he had shown my stash to a number of his friends and they were impressed by both its quantity and variety.

Acid Flashbacks On February 18, 1970, I began to experience acid flashbacks. I would see flashes and my head seemed to actually go into these trips – visually no, but mentally, yes! My mind was in very strange places....

Timothy Leary Many years later, on January 31, 1984, in Athens, Georgia, I had an opportunity to ask Timothy Leary the following question: "Do you accept responsibility for the thousands of people, both young and old, whose personalities were shattered as a result of following your prescription to drop acid?"

At first he denied that there were casualties. "There is no hard evidence that LSD and similar drugs have harmed anyone. No one was injured by their drug use." Looking him directly in the eye, I angrily interrupted, "We both know casualties from their drug use!"

Timothy Leary accepted my disagreement, saying, "Those who did have breakdowns could well have had them anyway; and besides, drinking and driving were a lot worse. When you're taking an evolutionary leap in consciousness, there will be some casualties. Every war has casualties.... Stupid people are going to use drugs stupidly. Intelligent people are going to use them intelligently. We're just going to have to raise the intelligence level."

(Throughout his life, Timothy Leary was very consistent in his belief that drugs would create an evolutionary leap in consciousness. Even as he was dying in 1996, he was reporting the effects of the drugs he was taking.)

Consciousness Research The field of consciousness research postulates that all humans have an innate desire to change their states of consciousness. We use substances or experiences to achieve this altered consciousness. It is a basic need. This fits nicely with yoga's assumption that all humans have an innate desire to be Self- and God-realized, to awaken to permanent liberation of consciousness.

Finding God-consciousness Through the years, my dream of expanded consciousness and spiritual growth through drugs evaporated. It was a dead end, leading nowhere. Psychedelic drugs were like a rocket ship. They would propel me to higher levels of consciousness, but, when the fuel ran out, when the drugs wore off, I found myself back on the ground and thoroughly spent.

My goal was to move to higher levels of consciousness and permanently live there, in God-consciousness. I found this impossible with drugs.

In addition, I ended up being hopelessly addicted to marijuana. It was not until June 17, 1985, that my addiction vanished. It was then that I was initiated into the Serenity Meditation. The depth of my meditation practice made further drug use superfluous.

I found that being high on drugs and alcohol interfered with my meditation practice. I could not do both and had to choose which was the most important to me. On one hand I had my drugs. On the other hand I had God-consciousness. **I chose God!**

Physiological and spiritual explanations clarify why my addiction to drugs magically evaporated when I began my meditation/prayer practice.

Physiological Explanation On a physiological level, I learned that my meditation/prayer practice elicited a relaxation response, which included a change of brain wave patterns.

When I studied the clinical research on addictions, I learned of one very interesting approach to treatment. This approach postulates that addicts are not actually addicted to their "drug of choice" but rather to Alpha, Theta, Delta, and Gamma brain waves.

Their "drug of choice" allows them to move from a predominately Beta brain wave pattern (active/anxious) to Alpha (relaxed), Theta (creative and intuitive), Delta (*yoga nidra* – mind awake, body asleep), and Gamma (superconsciousness, *Samadhi)* brain waves.

In meditation/prayer, brain wave patterns also alter from Beta to Alpha, Theta, Delta, and Gamma. Meditation/prayer literally rewires the brain. With practice, these changes become permanent. Drugs and alcohol are no longer needed or desired.

Spiritual Explanation I am convinced that, at their core, addictions are spiritual diseases. On a spiritual level, my meditation/prayer practice and God's grace allowed me to personally experience the Kingdom of God within me. The resulting bliss and peace left me feeling complete, whole. To my surprise, I discovered that my meditation practice not only freed me from drug addiction, but also eliminated all desire for alcohol.

I loved the state of consciousness I was in, the peace within me. My first priority became to protect my peace. Drugs and alcohol robbed me of my peace, and therefore had no place in my life. Meditation facilitated spiritual growth, which was the key to my recovery.

Caffeine Addiction and the Inner Sound Another addiction also evaporated as a result of my meditation practice -- my addiction to caffeine.

The Bible states, "In the beginning was the Word, and the Word was with God, and the Word was God" (John 1:1, KJV). In yoga, the Word is *Om* (Aum). The sound of *Om* is primordial, omnipresent, omnipotent, and omniscient.

I realize that most people do not consider caffeine to be a powerful drug or a problem. But my caffeine use kept me from hearing the inner sound of God, the sound of *Om*, which permeates the universe.

I discovered this quite by accident. During my seven- and ten-day retreats at Southern Dharma Retreat Center, caffeine was not available and, by the end of the retreat, I was clean, cleared of its effects. Over the years I learned that, when I was not on caffeine, I could hear the sound of *Om*, the sound of God. When I was on caffeine, I could not.

I also found listening to *Om*, the sound of God, to be very comforting, and strengthening. So once again I had a choice to make. On one hand I could have caffeine; on the other hand I could have the sound of God. It was an easy choice to make. **I chose God!**

> The evidential aspect of God is *Om*. [Sustained] meditation on *Om* culminates in knowledge of it and God-realization. – Yoga-sutra 1:27&29

Technique of Primordial Sound and Light Contemplation

I realize that some readers may wish to learn to listen to their inner sound, the sound of God, and see the inner light. Roy Eugene Davis, in his book, *Seven Lessons in Conscious Living* (CSA Press, 2013, pp. 56-58. Used with Permission) outlines the steps to follow to listen to your inner sound and see the inner light:

- Use your usual technique to meditate to the stage of tranquil, thought-free awareness.
- With your awareness at the spiritual eye center and higher brain, listen inside your ears and in your head until you discern a subtle sound. When a sound is heard, endeavor to hear a subtle sound behind it. Continue until you hear a sound that does not change.
- Blend your awareness with that sound. Merge in it.
- If you perceive inner light, blend your awareness with it as you merge your awareness with the sound.
- Gently inquire into the source of sound and light.
- Continue to meditate until you perceive that you are one with *Om* or until, having transcended it, you experience pure awareness of Being or a perception of oneness or wholeness.

The first sounds you hear may be those which occur naturally in the inner ear. As your attention becomes more internalized, you may discern the various subtle sound-frequencies of the vital centers (chakras) in the spinal pathway.

Eventually, when you hear a constant sound, use it as a mantra. Hear and perceive it in and outside of your head. Consider it as an aspect of *Om* which pervades your body and the universe. Expand and merge your awareness with it. If you perceive inner light, merge your awareness in it and *Om*.

Some meditators perceive a golden light, or a field of dark blue with a golden halo. They may also see a brilliant white light in the blue field. The teachers of this kriya yoga tradition declare golden light to be the radiance of *Om*; the dark blue to be the radiance of Consciousness-Intelligence that pervades the universe; and the brilliant white light to be the radiance of Consciousness itself.

If inner light is not easily perceived while contemplating *Om*, do not despair. Light perception, while of interest, is not as important as the clarification of awareness and the emergence of Self- and God-knowledge. Light perception is more likely when the waves of thoughts and emotions are pacified and remain dormant.

Any subjective perception of mental imagery (of people or other kinds of images) should be disregarded. The purpose of meditation practice is to transcend such phenomena. They are indications that desires, restlessness, and tendencies arising from the subconscious level of the mind are still influential. Be alert and attentive when meditating, yet patient as you learn by practice to acquire control of your attention and your states of awareness.

> I am dyed in the color of the Lord's name [*Om*],
> In a hue that can never fade;
> There is no color in the world
> That can be compared to the Lord's name. (Kabir)

Behavioral Medicine Applications

From July 4 – 8, 1994, I attended a training class on Behavioral Medicine Applications in Cape Cod, Massachusetts. It was taught by Herbert Benson, M.D., Alice Domar, Ph.D., and Ann Webster, Ph.D.

Herbert Benson's use of the term "relaxation response" really appealed to me. It was a neutral term, a Western, science-based concept that was easily accepted by the people with whom I was working. It simplified my presentations to groups representing a variety of religious affiliations.

Many of the conservative, fundamentalist, Southern Appalachian folks got very nervous when I talked of meditation, mantra meditation, etc. Hearing talk of "eliciting the relaxation response by using a focus word or phrase" was much more acceptable to them. Generally, unless individuals are comfortable with the terms and concepts presented, they are unlikely to practice and learn relaxation skills.

The following are copies of some of the handouts I received during training. I have used them often in my work and have found them quite helpful:

The Relaxation Response

The mind/body model of health suggests that our modern world – with its stresses, strains, and incessant changes – causes or aggravates many of our symptoms. You cannot always change your environment, and in many cases may not want to. But what can you do about the stresses of modem life? One answer lies within you.

By learning to use your awareness and your mind, you can begin to control your physical reactions to stress. You can cultivate the ability to turn within to give yourself a respite – a chance to slow down, relieve tension and anxiety, and renew yourself. First let us examine the physiology of stress.

The *Fight-or-Flight* Response   The *fight-or-flight response,* also called the stress response, was first identified by Dr. Walter B. Cannon of the Harvard Medical School early in this century. It is a profound set of involuntary physiological changes that occur whenever we are faced with a stressful or threatening situation. This response, critical to the survival of primitive humankind, prepares the body for a physical reaction to a real threat – to fight or flee.

Today, however, we do not often face the life threatening situations that primitive people responded to frequently, and the fight-or-flight response cannot distinguish between a serious threat and the everyday stresses of modern life. In fact, simply recalling a threatening or frightening situation is often enough to trigger the fight-or-flight response.

The fight-or-flight response is an integrated reaction controlled by the hypothalamus, an area of the brain. Confronted by a threat – physical or emotional, real or imagined – the hypothalamus causes the sympathetic nervous system to release epinephrine and norepinephrine (also called adrenaline and noradrenaline) and other related hormones. When rapidly released into the body, these powerful messengers propel you into a state of arousal. Your metabolism, heart rate, blood pressure, breathing rate, and muscle tension all increase.

Recently, researchers studying the long-term effects of the fight-or-flight response have concluded that it may lead to permanent, harmful physiological changes. The fight-or-flight response is useful and, in fact, necessary in times of emergency. But the stressors of modern living elicit it at times when it is inappropriate for us to run or fight. We must find ways to control the harmful aspects of this primitive physiological response and so neutralize the negative effects of modern stress on our health and well-being. The relaxation response can do just that.

The Counterbalancing Relaxation Response As demonstrated by researchers around the world and suggested by age-old wisdom, there is a *counterbalancing mechanism* to the fight-or-flight response. Just as stimulating an area of the hypothalamus can cause the stress response, so reducing the stimulation results in relaxation. The relaxation response is an inborn set of physiological changes that offset those of the fight-or-flight response. These changes are coordinated; they occur together in an integrated fashion.

The physiological changes of the fight-or-flight response and the relaxation response are polar opposites. In the fight-or-flight response, metabolism, heart rate, blood pressure, and muscle tension all **increase**. In the relaxation response, metabolism, heart rate, blood pressure, and muscle tension all **decrease**.

If the stresses of modern life cause the fight-or-flight response, the relaxation response can be used to counteract the harmful effects of stress. Just as the heart begins to beat rapidly when you imagine a frightening situation, your mind can be used to slow your heart rate.

There is one other significant difference between the fight-or-flight response and the relaxation response – the fight-or-flight response usually occurs involuntarily, whereas conscious elicitation of the relaxation response most often needs to be practiced.

(Worksheet adapted from *The Wellness Book: The Comprehensive Guide to Maintaining Health and Treating Stress-related Illness* (pp. 33-38), courtesy of Benson-Henry Institute for Mind Body Medicine, www.bensonhenryinstitute.org)

Learning to Elicit the Relaxation Response

The relaxation response is a state of profound rest that can have lasting effects throughout the day if you practice it regularly. What is relaxation? Many of us use the image of "letting go."

Physically, we mean releasing muscles from habitual, unconscious tension. We try to breathe more slowly and regularly, letting go of tension with each outbreath. Emotionally, we mean cultivating an attitude of greater equanimity. Mentally, we mean observing and letting go of troubling, worrisome thoughts. All of us can experience an enhanced ability to relax as we practice these different approaches to letting go.

Many people have difficulty relaxing their bodies: you think you are relaxed, when, in fact, your neck muscles are still tense. Cultivating a state of quiet acceptance in a world that demands so much is a new experience for many of us. To use an automotive image, shifting down from overdrive can be difficult for those accustomed to the fast lane. Yet, to restore a healthy balance, your body and mind need exactly such a change in pace.

To elicit the physiological state called the relaxation response, you need to develop techniques that help you "let go" more deeply than most of us can without such help. Remember that the relaxation response is a physiological response inborn to everyone, and it can occur at times when you are not even aware of it.

Bring to mind, for example, a time when you were lying on the beach on a warm summer day or moments at night when you drift into sleep. In both instances, the relaxation response is believed to account for the pleasant state and its measurable physiological changes. You can develop your innate ability to use these techniques in the most beneficial ways possible.

The relaxation response can be elicited by a number of techniques that involve mental focusing. All of these techniques have two basic components: the first is the *repetition* of a word, sound, phrase, prayer, image, or physical activity; the second is the *passive disregard of everyday thoughts* when they occur during relaxation.

As you try the different methods of eliciting the relaxation response, you may find that one method works better than others or that one or two of the techniques prove to be the most helpful. Or you may choose to make a combination of all the techniques part of your personal health regimen.

Find your own balance. Bear in mind that the goals of eliciting the relaxation response are straightforward, practical, and potentially transformative. Those who practice eliciting the relaxation response commonly report these kinds of changes:

- decrease in stress-related physical symptoms
- decrease in anxiety
- freedom from compulsive worrying, self-criticism
- increase in concentration and awareness
- improved sleep
- greater self-acceptance
- enhanced performance and efficiency

Spirituality Research studies confirm that such changes can occur with regular elicitation of the relaxation response. In addition, a recent study of the relationship between spirituality and health conducted by Jard Kass, Ph.D., and colleagues at Boston's Deaconess Hospital, found that a significant number of those who regularly elicit the relaxation response, regardless of method, reported an increase in positive attitudes associated with spirituality.

Spirituality in this study was linked to increased life purpose and satisfaction. They also found that increases in positive attitudes contributed to improvements in health. Regular elicitation of the relaxation response cultivated health-promoting attitudes which decreased the frequency of medical symptoms.

People who regularly elicit the relaxation response generally begin to describe themselves as more peaceful, energetic, self-accepting, happier, and so forth. Less preoccupied with past and future, they learn to enjoy the present moment more fully. In short, whatever their cultural or spiritual tradition, people can enjoy the benefits of the relaxation response in whatever way is most appropriate for them.

(Worksheet adapted from *The Wellness Book: The Comprehensive Guide to Maintaining Health and Treating Stress-related Illness* (pp. 33-38), courtesy of Benson-Henry Institute for Mind Body Medicine, www.bensonhenryinstitute.org)

Relaxation Response Instructions

1. Sit in a comfortable place but try not to lie down. If you lie down on your bed, chances are you will fall asleep. You may sit in a chair, on the floor with a cushion against the wall, or on the bed with a pillow behind you. If you must lie down, then the floor is recommended.

2. It is much easier to elicit the Relaxation Response (RR) in the same place each day. Try reserving that place for your relaxation; you will find that you will start to relax simply by sitting there. Make sure that the phone is unplugged, the door is closed, and your pets are absent (pets are strangely attracted to a relaxed person!).

3. It is also easier to elicit the RR at the same time(s) each day. This helps make it a habit.

4. If you are eliciting the RR on your own (i.e. not with a tape), do not set a timer. Sit opposite a clock and when you think that the time is up, slowly get up. If the time is

not up, simply close your eyes and go back to what you were focusing on.

5. It is quite normal for thoughts to come and go as you elicit the RR. Simply note that your mind has wandered, passively ignore the thoughts, and go back to what you were focusing on.

6. If you regularly exercise, try eliciting the RR immediately after you exercise; the sense of deep relaxation should come more easily.

7. Try not to elicit the RR either when you are very hungry or when you are full. Try having a glass of juice or a piece of fruit if you are hungry before sitting down. Wait a couple of hours after a full meal.

We generally advise eliciting the RR twice a day for 20 minutes each session. If you simply cannot fit in a session, try focusing on your breath for even five minutes. The only "bad RR" is one not done.

(Worksheet, courtesy of the Benson-Henry Institute for Mind Body Medicine, www.bensonhenryinstitute.org)

Focus Word or Phrase

The most universal methods of focusing your mind are linked to breathing, either by concentrating on your breathing itself or using it in conjunction with a focus word. Your focus word or mantra can be a word, phrase, or short prayer. "Mantra" means "the word that protects." When your mind is focused, you cannot dwell on negative, anxious thoughts.

A mantra has been a part of meditation and prayer in both Eastern and Western cultures for thousands of years. It is an anchor that helps you to quiet the self-talk chatter of your mind as you begin to meditate and pray.

Choosing your focus word is an important personal step. Tailor your focus word to your personal beliefs. This is often the best way to get maximum benefit from the relaxation response. If your focus word has special meaning, it will not only be more effective in meditation and prayer, but also you will likely become more deeply involved in practicing the relaxation response. The combination of the relaxation response with a personal belief system is sometimes called "the faith factor."

Some, however, prefer their focus word to have no connection to a belief system and choose a more neutral word or phrase. It may be meaningless, without any emotion or intellectual associations. It is usually a soothing, pleasant sound that has no sharp or irritating characteristics. Regardless of the particular word or phrase chosen, it is a key to eliciting the relaxation response through meditation and prayer.

Keep the word or phrase short enough to coordinate easily with your breath. The list below offers a range of focus words or phrases from which to choose. Choose one that most appeals to you or create your own if you prefer.

(Worksheet, from *The Wellness Book: The Comprehensive Guide to Maintaining Health and Treating Stress-related Illness*, courtesy of the Benson-Henry Institute for Mind Body Medicine, www.bensonhenryinstitute.org)

Common Focus Words or Phrases

General
*One   Peace   Calm   Let go   Relax   Light   Ocean
Oh well   Let it be   My time   Love Joy*

Christian
*God   Come, Lord   Lord, have mercy   Our Father
Our Father, who art in heaven   Jesus Saves*

*Lord Jesus Christ, Son of God, have mercy on me (a
sinner).
Lord Jesus Christ, have mercy on me.   Hail Mary
The Lord is my shepherd   Abba ("Father")*

Jewish
*Sh'ma Yisroel ("Hear, o Israel") Echod ("One")
Shalom ("Peace") Hashem ("The Name")*

Eastern
*Om (the universal sound)   Hong-sau
Shantih ("Peace")   So-ham*

Aramaic
Maranatha ("Come, Lord")

Islamic
Allah

(Worksheet, from *The Wellness Book: The Comprehensive
Guide to Maintaining Health and Treating Stress-related Illness,*
courtesy of the Benson-Henry Institute for Mind Body Medicine,
www.bensonhenryinstitute.org)

"Mini" Relaxation Exercises

Mini relaxation exercises are focused breathing
techniques which help reduce anxiety and tension
immediately!

You can do them with your eyes open or closed (but
make sure that your eyes are open when you are
driving!).

You can do them any place, at any time; no one will know
that you are doing them.

Ways to "do a mini"

Switch over to diaphragmatic breathing; if you are having
trouble, try breathing in through your nose and out

through your mouth, or take a deep breath. You should feel your stomach rising about an inch as you breathe in, and falling about an inch as you breathe out. If this is still difficult for you, lie on your back or on your stomach. You will be more aware of your breathing pattern.

Remember, it is impossible to breathe diaphragmatically if you are holding your stomach in! So... relax you stomach muscles.

Mini Version 1
Count very slowly to yourself from ten down to zero – one number for each breath. Thus, with the first diaphragmatic breath, you say "ten" to yourself; with the next breath, you say "nine," etc. If you start feeling light-headed or dizzy, slow down the counting. When you get to "zero," see how you are feeling. If you are feeling better, great! If not, try doing it again.

Mini Version 2
As you inhale, count very slowly up to four; as you exhale, count slowly back down to one. Thus, as you inhale, you say to yourself "one, two, three, four;" as you exhale, you say to yourself "four, three, two, one." Do this several times.

Mini Version 3
After each inhalation, pause for a few seconds; after you exhale, pause again for a few seconds. Do this for several breaths.

Good times to "do a mini"...
While being stuck in traffic ... when put on "hold" during an important phone call ... while waiting in your doctor's waiting room ... when someone says something which bothers you ... at all red lights ... when waiting for a phone call ... in the dentist's chair ... when you feel overwhelmed by what you need to accomplish in the near future ... while standing in line ... when in pain ... etc., etc.

THE ONLY TIME THAT MINIS DO NOT WORK IS WHEN YOU FORGET TO DO THEM!!! So go do a mini! ... .

(Worksheet, from *The Wellness Book: The Comprehensive Guide to Maintaining Health and Treating Stress-related Illness,* courtesy of the Benson-Henry Institute for Mind Body Medicine, www.bensonhenryinstitute.org)

Restitution – Working the Steps

Through my work with drug and alcohol addicts, I became familiar with Alcoholics Anonymous' Twelve Steps to recovery. I was impressed by the spiritual awakening the Twelve Steps invoked as addicts I knew "worked the steps." In January, 1995, I made the decision to follow their examples and "work the steps" in my own life, focusing on Step Eight and Step Nine.

Following Step Eight, I decided to "make a list of all persons I had harmed, and became willing to make amends to them all." After a life review, I remembered five instances where I had taken things that were not freely given to me. These five included a sleeping bag, items from a department store, training equipment, sound suppressant headphones, and video tapes.

Following Step Nine, I "made direct amends to such people wherever possible, except when to do so would injure them or others." (*Alcoholics Anonymous*, 3rd edition, 1976, p. 59.) Though difficult and <u>very</u> embarrassing, I telephoned each of the five places, told them what I had done, apologized for my behavior, and asked them how I could best make amends.

In some instances, I returned the stolen item; in others, I reimbursed. Throughout this process, I was often quite disconcerted and contrite. Thankfully, the folks I spoke with were extremely kind and very gracious to me. One even described me as the "nice man" who called; another ended our conversation by saying, "God Bless You."

Integral Yoga® Teacher Training

When I began my yoga practice, my meditation practice immediately deepened. In fact, the impact was so profound that I resolved to become a yoga teacher and share this jewel of yoga with others. After all, I had discovered meditation as the key to entering the Kingdom of God within, and anything that deepened meditation practice was precious knowledge and demanded to be shared with all!

From the many yoga training programs available, I chose Integral Yoga® teacher training. Every Integral Yoga® class included meditation. I knew that some yoga teacher training programs dealt only superficially with meditation. Some ignored meditation altogether.

In the West, yoga had been de-spiritualized! The most important part, the heart of yoga, was often ignored. Only the postures, the *asanas,* were emphasized. Integral Yoga® integrated four major practices, *asanas* (postures)*, pranayama* (breath control)*, yoga nidra* (deep relaxation), and meditation, into every class. I wanted to learn a balanced approach, an approach that included the jewel of meditation.

Once I decided which teacher training program to enter, I fearfully completed the application form. I write "fearfully" because I was applying to a program that would require me to use my body. Swami Satchidananda advised yogis to be "easeful and peaceful" in their body and mind. Unfortunately, during my lifetime I had rarely been easeful or peaceful!

I had always been overweight, usually obese. In 1972, I was in an industrial accident that permanently damaged my lower back. In 1991, I was rear-ended in a car wreck, which damaged my neck, my upper spine. Vertebral analysis indicated severely degenerated discs with bulges at 5C-6C and 4L-5L. Often in pain, I spent much time in a reclining chair or in bed. In short, physically I was a poor candidate for yoga teacher training.

I dedicated myself to God's service, and drove to Buckingham, Virginia, the home of Yogaville. I prayed to Divine Mother, acknowledging that only She could lead me to success in this endeavor. With Her support, I stayed in Yogaville for a month, from July 26 to August 24, 1997.

By August 1st, my back and neck hurt so much that I developed severe headaches which lasted for hours. It was embarrassing but I had to lie down during yoga class sessions, so great was my pain.

I wondered how long it would take before I healed. The last time I felt that injured was six years earlier. Then it seemed to take me forever to heal. I was trying to live in the present moment and not worry about what I could not control. I wished I was better at living that way all the time.

Pain was interesting. When it was not too overpowering, I could make it my focus of meditation and observe it as it came and went. This observation often lessened not the pain but the suffering that arose when I tried to push the pain away. Observing allowed me to be a witness to the pain, not trying to change it but to just accept it.

I had such difficulty mastering this material. Teacher training taught me how much of a stranger I was to my own body. I was completely out of touch with how to tell others to do the *asanas* because I was completely out of touch with my body.

Compounding this was the difficulty I found trying to teach poses I myself could not do because of my spinal cord injuries. I feared I would never be a very good yoga teacher. I reminded myself quite frequently that I was only learning to teach yoga so that I might serve others. My own meditation/prayer practice deepened when I began my Hatha Yoga, and I knew this would also be true for others.

Union with God Throughout my life, I had hoped to experience God-realization with a living teacher, one still in body. On August 17th, I did. After lunch, I went up to Swami Satchidananda with my newly purchased *mala* (prayer beads) and asked him to bless them.

As I knelt in front of him, he took the beads in his hands, closed his eyes, and said a long prayer. I closed my eyes for a few seconds and opened them expecting his prayer to be over. Instead Swami Satchidananda continued praying, eyes closed, continued to bless my *mala*, continued to bless me.

I stared into that wondrous form and felt such a power there. Just being that close to him for so long was <u>so</u> wonderful! I have never known such power from a living being. I could feel my heart as it seemed to swell with love until it was like a blown bud bursting with joy!

This transfer of *kundalini shakti*, cosmic power, love, from him to me struck me like a bolt of lightning. I thought he would just bless my beads; I did not know he would bless <u>*ME*</u>! I could hardly see; I could hardly walk. One staff member later said, "You had quite a transfer of *shakti*." My roommate said, "I saw the blessing you received. You are <u>very</u> lucky."

I felt lucky – I felt blessed!!!

In a daze I walked into the woods. Tears filled my eyes and I stumbled, twisting my ankle. Walking on, I found a quiet place by a stream and wept deeply. As I wept, I could feel my heart continue to open. The weeping came not from sorrow but from *immense **JOY!!!***

My *mala* even smelt differently. It smelled of him, of his radiance, of his beauty. Surely this was God dwelling among us! I had never been with a human being who was so filled with the Holy Spirit.

In the years since, I have never been quite the same. The doors to my heart had been flung open, leaving my heart overflowing with love. I now know that is how God intended I should live. I am forever grateful to Swami Satchidananda and God's love, which flowed through him.

God is Peace and Happiness Within After this wonderful experience with Swami Satchidananda, I began to seriously study his teachings:

> How can you look for God without knowing what God is? Can you look for a rose without knowing what a rose is? Even if you're surrounded by roses, if you don't know what a rose is, how are you going to recognize it? So, you should know what you are looking for even before you begin to look. That's why we say, in plain language, what you call, "God," is the peace and happiness in you. As peace and happiness, God is in you always. Recognize that and don't run after that from outside because it's not something that has to come from outside. "God made man in His own image," the Bible says. That means you are not even the body. You are the spirit. Therefore you don't have to look for your happiness from outside. You don't need anything to make you happy. (Used with Permission)

If the Kingdom of God is the peace and happiness within me, then protecting my peace must be my highest priority. I adopted this teaching as my own and try to live it daily.

I Passed!!! "Timings were perfect! This was a very nice beginners' Hatha Yoga class. Very smooth." These were my monitor's comments after observing my one and one-half hour class.

I was tired but very pleased to return home a successful graduate. I had arrived in Yogaville four weeks earlier, and the experience had been life altering. My heart felt more open, more alive. I was very thankful!

The following information I found interesting and useful:

Yoga Philosophy
(Used with Permission)

Eastern philosophy and psychology teach that the human psyche is veiled with many layers of ignorance that obscure our ability to see the Divine within us. However, at the deepest levels of being, we search for ways to re-establish our connection with our spiritual nature. For this reason, according to Eastern wisdom, we take on a human form.

Our activities while on Earth help us to work through the layers of ignorance, one by one. Finally, after much time and experience, we come to understand the true meaning of Self. In the moment of Self-realization, the ego is made free – free from the weight of all its illusions and free to reach its eternal destiny.

In this context, the body is a temple and also an instrument that allows us to experience life. A musician regularly tunes his instrument to improve its performance, cleaning and preparing it in a series of movements that look to us like little rituals. Similarly, taking care of the body is a ritualistic tuning by which we grow and perfect ourselves.

Regular exercise can do more than establish good health and a youthful appearance. When practiced with a devotional attitude, as a form of worship, physical activity keeps us in tune with life's purpose. Worship means devotion to something we love, admire, and respect. By exercising the body we show respect for the physical instrument that houses the spirit.

We should never begin a routine of physical exercise because we want to be superior to others in strength, or beauty. Sometimes, the more we become accomplished in life's activities, the more our ego is inflated. We see ourselves as masterful and, therefore, better than others.

There are two motivations for any activity in life. We can improve ourselves at the expense of others and obstruct our own growth, or we can improve our surroundings, help others to improve and, thereby, expand ourselves. As we develop more physical and mental balance and strength we participate more fully in creating healthier societies and environments and, finally, a healthier planet. Of all forms of movement, Yoga exercise ranks at the top because its purpose is to create balance in the body and mind.

Unfortunately, some people associate Yoga with mystical religions and cults. This misinterpretation of the science and philosophy of Yoga has discouraged many seekers of health who might, otherwise, benefit from this ancient practice.

We have found no other system that is as comprehensive and contributes as much to mind-body wellness as Yoga. The word "Yoga" means union. All exercises in Yoga, both physical and mental, are designed to unite the body with the mind and the individual self with the Self of all.

The physical exercises in Yoga, balance, stretch, tone, and strengthen the body in such a way that the nervous system and the mind can also be balanced and strengthened. Yoga exercises are based upon the premise that our mental and physical bodies work in synergy and that wherever there is synergistic harmony, there is health.

In Yoga there is no winning, or losing, and no competition with self, or others. Instead, all of our physical and mental activities become means to achieving the ultimate goal in life, the realization of our Divine Nature.

Integral Yoga®
(Used with Permission)

Integral Yoga is the synthesis of the various branches of Yoga. It is a scientific system for the harmonious development of every aspect of the individual. The following are some of its different branches.

HATHA YOGA: Predominantly concerned with the physical development, through asanas (postures), pranayama (breath control), deep relaxation, etc.

RAJA YOGA: Predominantly concerned with the control of the mind, through ethical perfection and regular practice of concentration and meditation.

BHAKTI YOGA: The path of devotion. By constant love, thought, and service of the Divine (either as God, a Divine Incarnation, or the spiritual teacher), the individual transcends his/her limited personality and attains Cosmic Consciousness. The path of Bhakti can be practiced by everyone. All that is needed is faith and constant remembrance of God.

JAPA YOGA: Japa Yoga is a part of Raja Yoga. Japa means repetition of a mantram. A mantram is a sound structure of one or more syllables which represents a particular aspect of the Divine Vibration. Concentrated mental repetition of the mantram produces vibrations within the individual's entire system which are in tune with the Divine Vibration.

KARMA YOGA: The path of action. By surrendering his/her individual will to the Cosmic Will, the practitioner becomes attuned to the freedom of his own actionless Self.

JNANA YOGA: The intellectual approach. Through the knowledge of what really exists, that is, what is not changeable, the Jnani (one who engages in the Path of Wisdom) realizes Oneness with the entire Universe.

(It is useful to remember that all these paths to God are equally valid; all lead to the same goal. "Paths are many; truth is one." Some personalities are better suited to a particular path. For example, I am drawn to *Bhakti Yoga*, the path of devotion.)

Raja Yoga: The Yoga of Meditation
(Used with Permission)

As a lamp placed in a windless spot does not flicker – to such is compared the Yogi of controlled mind, practicing Yoga in the Self (or absorbed in the Yoga of the Self). *Bhagavad Gita*, 6.19

In the study of Raja Yoga no faith or belief is necessary. Believe nothing until you find it out for yourself – that is what it teaches us. Truth requires no prop to make it stand.
Raja Yoga, Swami Vivekananda

Yoga means union. Union with the Divine is the ultimate aim. Raja Yoga is the royal path, for Raja means king. Raja Yoga deals with the mind directly and is, therefore, called the Kingly Yoga. It is also called Ashtanga Yoga, ashtanga meaning eight-fold. There are eight steps in the ladder of Raja Yoga. These are:

1.   YAMA (Restraints)

a. Ahimsa (harmlessness, non-violence)
b. Satya (truthfulness)
c. Brahmacharya (continence)
d. Asteya (non-stealing, non-covetousness)
e. Asparigraha (non-hoarding)

2.   NIYAMA (Observances)

a. Saucha (purity, internal and external)
b. Santosha (contentment)
c. Tapas (austerity)
d. Svadhyaya (spiritual study)
e. Ishwarapranidhana (self-surrender to the Lord)

3.   ASANA (Physical posture)

4.   PRANAYAMA (Breath regulation)

5.   PRATYAHARA (Withdrawing of the senses)

6.   DHARANA (Concentration on one point)

7.   DHYANA (Meditation, the steady flow of thought upon one point)

8.   SAMADHI (Absorption, subject and object become one)

[Note that the *Yamas* (Restraints) and *Niyamas* (Obervances) form the foundation practices. That is, success is unlikely without living the *Yamas* and *Niyamas*. *Samadhi,* union with God, is improbable.]

Koshas
(Used with Permission)

(There are five sheaths to us, covering the Atman or true self, which is unchanging and eternal.)

ANAMAYA KOSHA – PHYSICAL SHEATH.
Has six expressions: EXISTENCE, BIRTH, GROWTH, MODIFICATION, DECAY, DEATH.
It is a tool to enhance awareness.

PRANAMAYA KOSHA – VITAL ENERGY SHEATH
Contains prana or vital energy of self. Can be controlled with the breath. It is the link between body and mind, and

we can use it to control the mind. This is the level of the aura, chakras and nadis (meridians).

MANOMAYA KOSHA – MENTAL SHEATH
Consists of perceptual organization, habits, language, and emotions. It is connected to the senses. Fears and desires are part of the Manomaya Kosha, also acting impulsively.

VIJNANAMAYA KOSHA – INTELLECTUAL SHEATH
Discrimination, the ability to discern.   The witness. Critical thinking, cause/effect relations.
Sometimes a battle between the Manomaya Kosha and the Vijnanamaya Kosha. "I know I shouldn't, but I want to." (from fears and desires).

ANANDAMAYA KOSHA – BLISS SHEATH
Experience of inner harmony and peace. Intuition. Absolute self-confidence; equanimity, sense of well-being.
Balanced mind leads to Anandamaya Kosha

ATMAN – TRUE SELF
One with all. The True Witness.
The Pranamaya through Anandamaya Koshas compose the human soul. They continue on after the body dies and eventually take another birth.

[If one can truly "let go" during *yoga nidra* (deep relaxation) and meditation, consciousness, "the witness", will move from *Anamaya Kosha* (Physical Sheath) to Pranamaya *Kosha* (Vital Energy Sheath) to *Manomaya Kosha* (Mental Sheath) to *Vijnanamaya Kosha* (Intellectual Sheath) and rest in *Anandamaya Kosha* (Bliss Sheath). This is why *yoga nidra* (deep relaxation) and meditation are so powerful.

It can be extremely disconcerting to be suddenly disturbed while resting in *Anandamaya Kosha,* while resting in Bliss. The person can be thrown into confusion and lose all composure. For this reason, care and sufficient time should be taken when ending *yoga nidra* (deep relaxation) and meditation. From my own experiences, I have learned that it can be most unpleasant to suddenly terminate.

One instance was particularly disconcerting. On April 25, 2013, I was in retreat at Myrtle Beach, South Carolina. It was sunset and I was at the ocean, deep in meditative bliss consciousness. Someone I had talked with earlier came up behind me and violently boxed my ears. It was an abrupt and painful termination! The man later explained that he thought I was only sleeping. It actually took me several hours to recover from the experience.]

The Breath of Life
By Sri Swami Satchidananda
(Used with Permission)

Prana: The Vital Force When you breathe, in addition to the oxygen, you also take in a lot of prana. The oxygen gets diffused in the lungs and then gets into the bloodstream, but the prana goes throughout the body. It enters into every area – physical, vital and mental. Every cell of your body vibrates with new life.

Prana is our very life. It is the vital force that pervades the entire cosmos. You get prana from food, from the sun and from the air you breathe. You can live for many weeks without food, days without water, minutes without air, but not even for a fraction of a second without prana.

In Sanskrit, if you deify the prana you can call it Parashakti, the Cosmic Power. Wherever you see power, you see the action of prana. Even the movements in an atom are due to the prana within it. The light and heat in a flame are prana. Electricity is prana. Your motorcar moves with prana – gasoline is a liquid form of prana. To raise your hand you need prana. Your breathing is prana. Your digestion is prana. Even to think you need prana, because it is the subtle prana that moves the mind.

All movement everywhere is caused by prana, the cosmic energy. The entire nature is moving constantly. That is the nature of the nature – constant movement and transformation. And it is the prana that causes all the movement. So why should we want to control it?

Pranayama: Controlling the Cosmic Power In pranayama we are trying to handle and control the cosmic Shakti. Pranayama is composed of two words: "prana" and "ayama." "Ayama" means regulation, control, or mastery. We begin by regulating the prana that moves our own bodies and minds.

When we gain mastery over the prana, we have mastery over the inner nature, too, because it is the prana that creates all the movements in an individual – physical and mental. We try to control the inner nature, because it is the nature's movement that causes a lot of disturbance in the system and makes it impossible for the Light within to shine in its true, original way.

When we can control the prana inside, we can control the prana outside, too. They are one and the same force on different levels. The body is a microcosm, and the universe outside is a macrocosm. So, by the regular practice of pranayama, we are able not only to control and direct the prana that functions within us, but the universal prana as well.

Yogic Breathing With proper pranayama you begin to use the entire lungs. You take in much more than your normal quota of oxygen and prana. It can be measured in laboratory tests.

In normal breath, you inhale five hundred cubic centimeters of air, and then you breathe out the same. After your exhalation, the lungs are almost empty. Still, there is residual air in the lungs. After you breathe out your normal five hundred cubic centimeters, if you pull your tummy in slightly, you can exhale some more air, which has been measured as sixteen hundred cubic centimeters.

Now you begin to inhale. You first inhale the air that you squeezed out – sixteen hundred cubic centimeters. Then you inhale your normal five hundred. And then afterwards, you can inhale some additional air. If you inhale more deeply, you can take in another sixteen hundred cubic centimeters. So, after a complete squeezing out on the exhalation, you can inhale thirty-seven hundred cubic centimeters.

So, instead of your usual five hundred cubic centimeters, you can take in thirty-seven hundred cubic centimeters – more than seven times as much as in a normal breath. In every breath you can take in seven times more air, more oxygen, and more prana if you do the pranayama regularly.

Imagine the advantage. The quality of the blood improves and the richness of the blood is the basis of the entire body's health. Your blood gets more oxygenated. Oxygen is life. It is a great panacea, a fine medicine for all kinds of poisons. When you have that much vitality, no virus can even think of coming near you. As soon as it comes near you, burn it out. That is the beauty of pranayama.

Benefits of Pranayama   The main purposes of pranayama are to purify the system and to calm and regulate the mind. Pranayama purifies the nervous system and eliminates toxins from the body and blood.

It helps in the curing of asthma, consumption, and other respiratory disorders. With proper breathing, you can eliminate the excess mucous which causes most hay fever and sinus discomfort. You can exhilarate the blood circulation and stimulate the entire body quickly.

Pranayama produces lightness of body, alertness of mind, good appetite, proper digestion, and sound sleep.

Pranayama helps you to attain radiant health, but that is only a secondary benefit, a by-product, of the practice of pranayama. The main aim is to control the mind through the prana. If you can control the mind, you are the master. The prana – here as the movement of the breath – and the movement of the mind – go together.

If you regulate the prana, you have regulated, through the movement of the breath, that same pranic movement in the mind. Should you ever feel upset, tense, or worried, do some slow deep breathing with full attention on the breath, and you will easily bring the mind to a calm state.

According to the *Yoga Sutras*, a veil of mental darkness covers the Light within. The benefit of pranayama is that it removes this veil, and the mind becomes clear and fit for concentration. So, pranayama is a beautiful preparation for meditation. Before meditation, do three rounds of Bastrika, the bellows breath. It will exhilarate the entire body, drive off drowsiness, remove tension, and bring harmonious movement in all the cells.

After this, do some alternate nostril breathing, or some slow, deep breathing through both nostrils at the same time. Follow the breath with the mind. Feel how it comes in, how far it goes, and how it returns. Calm, slow, and steady breathing will also keep the mind very calm.

To derive the maximum benefit, go slowly in developing your practice. Be patient. Pranayama should never be done in a hurry, nor should you try to advance too quickly, because you are dealing with vital energy.

The Yoga scriptures personify prana as a deadly cobra. So, remember you are playing with a cobra. If you play well and make the cobra dance, you will accrue many benefits, as did the snake charmers in India. They used their snakes for their livelihood. But if they didn't play properly, they would be killed. In the same way, with prana, you should be very careful. Do everything gently; avoid even the slightest strain, and never hurry.

Over the years, my students have consistently reported that one of the most beneficial lessons they have learned in my classes is *pranayama*, breath control. It is a technique they can use every day, wherever they are.

Those, who wake up during the night, successfully use it to go back to sleep, thus often gaining hours of additional sleep. Others use it throughout the day to help maintain balance, to be more peaceful and joyful. Experience has taught me not to underestimate the value of *pranayama*!

Sivananda Ashram Yoga Retreat

After leaving Yogaville in August, 1997, my back and neck continued to hurt, sometimes quite badly. The pain severely diminished the quality of my life, and I became desperate for relief. In late December, I learned that Amrita (Dr. Sandra McLanahan) was presenting programs in January at the Sivananda Ashram Yoga Retreat. The ashram is located on Paradise Island, just off Nassau in the Bahamas.

I telephoned Amrita while she was still in Yogaville, Virginia, and told her of my pain. I asked her if she would work with me if I came to Paradise Island while she did her program at Sivananda Ashram. She agreed to help me, and added, "The reason to work on this body is so you will be around long enough to be able to evolve to a higher state of consciousness."

Amrita and Fasting When I arrived on Paradise Island, I met with Amrita and reviewed the many things I had done to alleviate my pain. She listened intently. Since my body had not healed itself during these many months following yoga boot camp in Yogaville, Amrita suggested that I give my body less to do. I needed to allow my body to focus on healing itself, not digesting food.

Amrita told me not to eat anything but protein powder and fruit for the next ten days. I could eat all the fruit and protein powder I wanted during that period, but nothing else. She added that, if my tongue turned bright pink before the ten days expired, I should begin to eat normally. She explained that, when the tongue turned bright pink, it indicated that the body had consumed all the *ama*, the undigested material. If the modified fast continued past this point, the body would begin to consume muscle.

At her direction, I went into Nassau to buy protein powder and an enema bag. Amrita said it was important that I have a bowel movement, however small, every day. If I went a day without a bowel movement, the next day I should use the enema bag and give myself an enema. (Thankfully, I never needed to use the bag.)

Amrita also suggested taking advantage of the many healing modalities available at the ashram. She hoped, by doing so, that I would discover some effective strategies for alleviating my pain.

It had been many years since I went without food. By the end of the first day, I was nauseous and <u>extremely</u> light headed. In the evening, I asked Amrita if I could die. She just smiled and assured me that I would not die.

By the next morning, I felt so bad that I wished I had died! I told my roommate, as he left our cabin, to lock the door and leave me in my private hell. I skipped morning meditation and hatha and just lay there, unable to move. Periodically, during the day, I would sip my soy powder and pineapple juice in hopes of clearing my head and settling my stomach.

The next afternoon I finished some broth, which warmed me up and made me feel <u>great</u>! Amrita suggested that, as my blood sugar level was so high – 92 that morning – my feeling terrible had more to do with toxins being released from the body.

It had taken me about three hours each morning to feel human, and I felt pretty good that day, especially considering it had been three days since I last ate. So far this trip to the Bahamas had been most interesting.

With Amrita's assistance, I finally discovered a treatment modality that worked on my pain. A woman from Israel had me lie on the floor, put my head in her lap, and rocked me cuddled in her arms. MY PAIN DISAPPEARED!!!

I was very excited to finally discover a way to relieve my pain! But, unfortunately, her guru told her to have no contact with men, so she refused to give me further treatments. (When I returned home, I put hammocks along Panther Brook. The swinging motions while lying down helped ease pain, and made longer meditation periods possible.)

On my fourth day of fasting I noticed that I was hungry, that I wanted to eat food more than at any time since beginning the fast. My room was located across from the kitchen and the smells were really making me HUNGRY!!! I was definitely looking forward to broth at dinner!

Later, I had my broth – lots of it – and it was every bit as good as I hoped. The vegetables look beautiful in the pot cooking, really beautiful! Unfortunately, of course, I could not eat any. I will always remember lusting after one particularly beautiful ear of corn, forbidden corn.

I was having such a good time at the ashram. I attended a meditation workshop and introduced myself this way (We were instructed to use only three sentences.): "I am pure light. I am beautiful. Divine Mother sings through me."

On the 15th of January, Amrita took me to the hot tub at the Sheraton. On the way, I stepped on an old wooden post and tore a good thick layer of skin off my foot. Amrita's reaction was noteworthy. She said, "God really loves you. He wants you to burn all your karma in this lifetime."

Amrita believed in a lawful universe. This was such an attractive concept to me. She had such wonderful <u>faith</u>, was a being of pure light, a being with a wonderful, generous spirit! I could feel Divine Mother moving through her. I felt that way when we first met at Yogaville, and my time with her on Paradise Island further confirmed it.

And so I hobbled to the hot tub and it was <u>so</u> nice – a <u>beautiful</u> experience in a magnificent setting. We then swam in the Treasure Island pool, swimming all the way around the island. The next day Amrita flew back to Yogaville.

On January 19th, I woke up <u>not</u> feeling sick, as if I were going to die. For the first time since my fast began, I actually made the morning meditation. Apparently, I had <u>so</u> many toxins in me that it took <u>seven</u> days to rid myself of them. Amazing!!!

Before she left, Amrita told me to fast for no more than ten days, or until my tongue turned pink – whichever occurred first. My tongue remained coated with an ugly, grayish white substance – undigested *ama*, I presumed.

Tears were close to the surface. Periodically, I cried. I seemed to have a well of sorrow that emerged, bursting forth as I quieted the mind and purified the body.

At this point in my fast, I resolved to continually chant my mantra, both day and night. Every conscious moment I chanted "Om – Shanti, Om – Shanti, Om – Shanti, Om – Shanti, Om – Shanti, Om – Shanti …"

I chose "Om – Shanti" as my mantra, mentally chanting "Om" as I breathed in and "Shanti" as I breathed out. This was a mantra suggested by Swami Satchidananda, and loosely translated meant "God – Peace."

Pink Tongue On the eighth day my tongue turned a very bright **pink**!!! I was so happy, and the food I ate that day tasted like nectar! Each day at the ashram seemed so magical, so intense. Before she left, Amrita had suggested routinely fasting and maintaining silence one day each week, a practice I found very useful.

While exploring Atlantis, a large casino complex just down the beach from the ashram, I discovered a huge aquarium with many beautiful fish. I began visiting the fish every day, just sitting and watching. I also continued my daily visit to the hot tub, which helped make my neck and back pain quite bearable. (When I returned home, I began taking a hot tub bath daily, which continued to be an effective treatment for my pain.)

On February 4th I spent the day silently chanting my mantra, fasting, and maintaining silence. I had discovered that fasting and silence did go together! I chose that day for fasting and silence because the previous night I had cleared the food off my plate while talking way too much, hardly tasting my food. Fasting stopped the mindless eating process in its tracks and silence accentuated it. Together they made a very powerful combination.

Women I read a book by Sivananda titled *Kundalini*. He recommended staying away from all women. I understood and agreed with him totally, as there was an amazing assortment of beautiful women on Paradise Island. I looked forward to going home to my own ashram, Panther Brook Spiritual Center – one much quieter.

It was a quite a challenge to maintain my peace in the midst of so many beautiful women! When I was not chanting or meditating with the group, I would silently chant my mantra, "Om – Shanti," or listen to my inner sound, which was usually a beautiful, high tone.

Fasting seemed to increase the volume of my inner sound, and my meditations and continuous chanting raised the pitch. I had been told that the pitch of the inner sound corresponded to the chakra the individual operated from – the higher the pitch, the tone, the higher the chakra. This was another instance where I thought a concept to be intellectually interesting, but not provable. However, on Paradise Island, I lived it. I loved the volume and pitch of my inner sound, which often became an inner roar!

But Club Med was next to the ashram, and I had to walk through it on the way to my daily visit to the hot tub and fish. As I walked along the beach, there were usually several incredibly beautiful women wearing almost nothing. It seemed as though I met this one particular woman every day. She was generously endowed and had a very small piece of fabric covering each nipple and her vulva.

I was fascinated to hear my inner sound drop in pitch when I saw her. I could actually <u>hear</u> the change in pitch! These experiences convinced me that the various chakras <u>do</u> vibrate at different frequencies!

It became an interesting experiment for me to learn how to walk past these beautiful, almost naked women, and maintain a high pitch to my inner sound. I found citing my mantra actually helped me keep my inner sound at a sweet, high pitch! After all, "mantra" means the "word that protects!"

During my month on Paradise Island, I received training in visualization and relaxation techniques, meditation, and yoga. My stay increased my understanding and teaching skills in several areas of behavioral medicine. I also learned several strategies for alleviating my pain. These included silence and fasting, hot soaks in the tub, and swinging in a hammock.

When I left Paradise Island and headed for the airport, I sat in the cab's front passenger seat. While passing a large bus, the cab driver refused to retreat in the face of an oncoming car. I thought we were sure to crash and, without conscious thought, immediately began quickly, quietly chanting my mantra, "Om – Shanti." After a month of continuous practice, the mantra was <u>so</u> deeply ingrained that, in the face of death, it automatically came to protect me.

I was reminded of a story I heard about Mahatma Gandhi. When he was assassinated, the bullet struck him in his heart, exploding it and causing instantaneous death. On his last out breath, Gandhi's mantra spontaneously arose from his lips: "*Rama, Rama, Rama*". It was so deeply ingrained in him that it required no thought, no intention. "*Rama*" (God) protected him, shielding him from fear, even as he made his transition.

My First Christian Centering Prayer Retreat

On May 1 – 3, 1998, I attended my first Christian Centering Prayer retreat at Southern Dharma. The retreat was led by David Frenette, who became a Christian in 1981, after beginning his spiritual journey with Buddhist meditation. Beginning in 1984, David practiced and worked under the guidance of Abbot Thomas Keating.

This was my first formal introduction to Christian Centering Prayer and I was excited to discover and learn about a Christian meditative spiritual tradition. This reinforced my desire to be a follower of Christ. I also knew that Christian Centering Prayer would be more acceptable to the many Christians with whom I worked.

Not Teaching Religion but God-realization   I was not interested in teaching religion. What I wanted to teach was how to be closer to God, how to enter into the Kingdom of God! Each of us has this river of God's grace flowing beneath us. We need to dig a deep well to tap into this grace. If one is fortunate enough to have developed a heart connection to God during religious training in childhood, then that existing well should be dug deeper through meditation/prayer practice.

It makes no sense to change religions and start digging a brand new well. I am convinced that all religions, all meditation/prayer techniques, eventually bring the practitioner to the same place. "Truth is One; Paths are Many!" The challenge is to motivate the person to actually begin a meditation/prayer practice.

Father Thomas Keating is a founder of the Centering Prayer Movement and of Contemplative Outreach. (I am grateful for permission to use this material. For information about Contemplative Outreach, see www.contemplativeoutreach.org)

In *Open Mind, Open Heart,* Father Keating states, "There are all kinds of ways in which God speaks to us – through our thoughts or any one of our faculties. But keep in mind that God's first language is silence." (p. 57)

> The root of prayer is interior silence. We may think of prayer as thoughts or feelings expressed in words, but this is only one of its forms. ... Contemplative Prayer is not so much the absence of thoughts as detachment from them. It is the opening of mind and heart, body and emotions – our whole being – to God, the Ultimate Mystery, beyond words, thoughts, and emotions – beyond, in other words, the psychological content of the present moment. (p.14)

Father Thomas Keating explains that, through the regular practice of contemplative prayer, interior purification occurs. "This dynamism is a kind of divine psychotherapy, organically designed for each of us, to empty out our unconscious and free us from the obstacles to the free flow of grace in our minds, emotions, and bodies" (p. 93).

Through this divine psychotherapy, one moves from the "false self" to the "true self." Father Thomas Keating describes the "false self" and the "true self":

> **False Self** – the self developed in our own likeness rather than in the likeness of God; the self-image developed to cope with the emotional trauma of early childhood, which seeks happiness in satisfying the instinctual needs of survival/security, affection/esteem, and power/control, and which basis its self-worth on cultural or group identification.

> **True Self** – the image of God in which every human being is created; our participation in the divine life

manifested in our uniqueness. (Keating, T. (1992). *Open mind, open heart: The contemplative dimension of the Gospel.* New York, New York: Continuum. pp. 146-147.)

The Method of Christian Centering Prayer
(Used with Permission)

The Guidelines

1. CHOOSE A SACRED WORD AS THE SYMBOL OF YOUR INTENTION TO CONSENT TO GOD'S PRESENCE AND ACTION WITHIN.

2. SITTING COMFORTABLY AND WITH EYES CLOSED, SETTLE BRIEFLY AND SILENTLY INTRODUCE THE SACRED WORD AS THE SYMBOL OF YOUR CONSENT TO GOD'S PRESENCE AND ACTION WITHIN.

3. WHEN YOU BECOME AWARE OF THOUGHTS, RETURN EVER-SO-GENTLY TO THE SACRED WORD.

4. AT THE END OF THE PRAYER PERIOD, REMAIN IN SILENCE WITH EYES CLOSED FOR A COUPLE OF MINUTES.

Contemplative Prayer Contemplative Prayer is the normal development of the grace of baptism and the regular practice of *Lectio Divina*. [*Lectio Divina* is the reading and listening to biblical texts and is the most ancient method of developing the friendship of Christ.] We may think of prayer as thoughts or feelings expressed in words, but this is only one expression.

Contemplative Prayer is the opening of mind and heart – our whole being – to God, the Ultimate Mystery, beyond thoughts, words, and emotions. We open our awareness to God whom we know by faith is within us, closer than breathing, closer than thinking, closer than choosing – closer than consciousness itself. Contemplative prayer is a process of interior purification leading, if we consent, to divine union.

The Method Centering Prayer is a method designed to facilitate the development of contemplative prayer by preparing our faculties to cooperate with this gift

It is not meant to replace other kinds of prayer; it simply puts other kinds of prayer into a new and fuller perspective. During the time of prayer, we consent to God's presence and action within. At other times our attention moves outward to discover God's presence everywhere.

Explanation of the Guidelines

I. "Choose a sacred word as the symbol of your intention to consent to God's presence and action within." (cf. *Open Mind, Open Heart*, chap. 5)

1. The sacred word expresses our intention to be in God's presence and to yield to the divine action.

2. The sacred word should be chosen during a brief period of prayer asking the Holy Spirit to inspire us with one that is especially suitable to us.

a) Examples: Lord, Jesus, Father, Mother, Mary; or in other languages: Kyrie, Jesu, Jeshua, Abba, Mater, Maria.

b) Other possibilities: Love, Peace, Mercy, Silence, Stillness, Calm, Faith, Trust, Yes; or in other languages: Amor, Shalom, Amen.

3. Having chosen a sacred word, we do not change it during the prayer period, for that would be to start thinking again.

4. A simple inward gaze upon God may be more suitable for some persons than the sacred word. In this case, one consents to God's presence and action by turning inwardly to God as if gazing upon Him. The same guidelines apply to the sacred gaze as to the sacred word.

II. "Sitting comfortably and with eyes closed, settle briefly and silently introduce the sacred word as the symbol of your consent to God's presence and action within."

1. By "sitting comfortably" is meant relatively comfortably; not so comfortably that we encourage sleep, but sitting comfortably enough to avoid thinking about the discomfort of our bodies during the time of prayer.

2. Whatever sitting position we choose, we keep the back straight.

3. If we fall asleep, we continue the prayer for a few minutes upon awakening if we can spare the time.

4. Praying in this way after a main meal encourages drowsiness. Better to wait an hour at least before Centering Prayer. Praying in this way just before retiring may disturb one's sleep pattern.

5. We close our eyes to let go of what is going on around and within us.

6. We introduce the sacred word inwardly and as gently as laying a feather on a piece of absorbent cotton.

III. "When you become aware of thoughts, return ever-so-gently to the sacred word."

1. "Thoughts" is an umbrella term for every perception including sense perceptions, feelings, images, memories, reflections, and commentaries.

2. Thoughts are a normal part of Centering Prayer.

3. By "returning ever-so-gently to the sacred word", a minimum of effort is indicated. This is the only activity we initiate during the time of Centering Prayer.

4. During the course of our prayer, the sacred word may become vague or even disappear.

IV. "At the end of prayer period, remain in silence with eyes closed for a couple of minutes."

The additional 2 or 3 minutes give the psyche time to readjust to the external senses and enable us to bring the atmosphere of silence into daily life.

Some Practical Points

1. The minimum time for this prayer is 20 minutes. Two periods are recommended each day, one first thing in the morning, and one in the afternoon or early evening.

2. The end of the prayer period can be indicated by a timer, provided it does not have an audible tick or loud sound when goes off.

3. The principal effects of Centering Prayer are experienced in daily life, not in the period of Centering Prayer itself.

4. Physical Symptoms:

a. We may notice slight pains, itches, or twitches in various parts of the body or a generalized restlessness. These are usually due to the untying of emotional knots in the body.

b. We may also notice heaviness or lightness in the extremities. This is usually due to a deep level of spiritual attentiveness.

c. In either case, we pay no attention, or we allow the mind to rest briefly in the sensation, and then return to the sacred word.

5. *Lectio Divina* provides the conceptual background for the development of Centering Prayer.

6. A support group praying and sharing together once a week helps maintain one's commitment to the prayer.

Points for Further Development

1. During the prayer period various kinds of thoughts may be distinguished. (cf. *Open mind, open heart*, chap. 6-10):

a. Ordinary wanderings of the imagination or memory.
b. Thoughts that give rise to attractions or aversions.
c. Insights and psychological breakthroughs.
d. Self-reflections such as, "How am I doing?" or, "This peace is just great!"
e. Thoughts that arise from the unloading of the unconscious.

2. During this prayer we avoid analyzing our experience, harboring expectations or aiming at some specific goal such as:

a. Repeating the sacred word continuously.
b. Having no thoughts.

c. Making the mind a blank.
d. Feeling peaceful or consoled.
e. Achieving a spiritual experience.

3. What Centering Prayer is:

a. It is at the same time a relationship with God and a discipline to foster that relationship.
b. It is an exercise of faith, hope, and love.
c. It is a movement beyond conversation with Christ to communion.
d. It habituates us to the language of God which is silence.

Adapted from Keating, T. (1995). *The method of centering prayer*. Butler, NJ: Contemplative Outreach. Used with permission.

Keating, T. (1995). *Open mind. open heart*. New York, NY: Continuum. Used with permission.

Don't judge centering prayer on the basis of how many thoughts come or how much peace you enjoy. The only way to judge this prayer is by its long-range fruits: whether in daily life you enjoy greater peace, humility and charity. Having come to deep interior silence, you begin to relate to others beyond the superficial aspects of social status, race, nationality, religion, and personal characteristics. (Keating, T. (1995). *Open mind, open heart*. p. 114.)

Catastrophic Loss

I had taken time to heal from the great losses of my life. My grandmother, Nannie, who helped raise me and passed when I was twenty-four, was my first loss of magnitude. My father, who passed on the same day nineteen years later, was the second. My mother, who passed three years after him, was the third.

Leaving my position as psychology professor ranked alongside these other major losses of my life.

During the previous fifteen years, I had created a psychology program that was quite popular. More students majored in psychology than any other major in the School of Arts and Sciences. When I began my work at the college, less than one percent of the entire student body majored in psychology. When I retired, over ten percent of the entire student body majored in psychology. Now that I am no longer employed at the college, around one percent of the entire student body majors in psychology.

I thought I would continue to be of service to my college and its students, faculty, staff, and surrounding community for another fifteen years. Several psychology students who graduated from my program had stayed in touch and I rejoiced to hear of their successes. I established a scholarship fund in honor of my parents, which continues to award scholarships. I saw my life mission being fulfilled as a college professor of psychology.

I will not go into detail about how I lost my job except to say it became increasingly difficult to maintain my peace as my professional world changed around me. Protecting my peace is my highest priority. Over time, I realized that maintaining my peace was more important to me than my job. In the end, a powerful college president engineered my catastrophic loss.

I had such anger and hatred in my heart for this college president, and, the more my anger and hatred grew, the less I felt like the person I wanted to be. I wanted to live without enemies, to be Self-realized, feeling no separation between me and all living, sentient beings. I understood that my anger and hatred were not hurting the president; they were only hurting me.

Pratipaksha Bhavana I resolved to turn my anger and hatred into love, and used the yoga practice of *Pratipaksha Bhavana* to achieve that goal. There are two aspects to *Pratipaksha Bhavana:*

1.   If you have negative thoughts, substitute positive ones instead. Two contrary thoughts cannot occupy the mind at the same time. For example, when I am angry, my thoughts are angry. I can substitute thoughts of love and patience for thoughts of anger and hatred.

2.   Contemplate; reflect upon the negative consequences of negative behavior.   And, after reflecting, abstain from the negative behavior. For example, when I want to do something which I know will cause great pain, I can reflect upon the negative consequences of that behavior and not do it.

I placed a picture of the college president on my altar and every day practiced a loving kindness meditation while looking at his picture.

May you be peaceful and happy.
May you be free from suffering.
May you be filled with love.
May you be free.

I also frequently talked to his picture, wishing him a good day, etc. It took a long time and I often did not want to do it, but eventually my anger and hatred turned to love. Once again I lived without anger and hatred in my heart, lived without enemies.

The college president was the greatest spiritual teacher I ever had. Because of all the pain, I was forced to spiritually grow. I am not the only person to spiritually grow from great upheaval. His Holiness the Dalai Lama was once asked, "Who was your greatest spiritual teacher?" Without hesitation, he responded, "Mao."

Admittedly, if I had not been through the ordeal with the college president, I could never have written and released this spiritual autobiography. But the loss of my job allowed me to see how shallow and ultimately meaningless that which I considered important really was. I have learned that the only important, lasting thing is how I feel inside of <u>ME</u>.

Intermediate Hatha Yoga Teacher Training

From June 25 – July 8, 2000, I attended Intermediate Hatha Yoga Teacher Training in Yogaville, Virginia. Many of the *asanas* were difficult to learn because my spine precluded me from doing them.

God Enters my Heart On June 29th, we began class by chanting "Door of my Heart," written by Paramahansa Yogananda. [Yogananda, P. (1974). *Cosmic chants.* Los Angeles, CA: Self-Realization Fellowship. p. 23]

I am not certain when I began to think that I should chant, sing loudly, with great gusto, so God can clearly hear me. Perhaps I think God has so much to do that I need to make myself noticed. Perhaps I just think God is hard of hearing. But, over my lifetime, I have discovered that, when I sing with great enthusiasm, my heart opens. I have learned that it is best to sing, not from the head or throat, but from the heart!

I sang <u>loudly</u>, as though commanding my heart to open to God's presence – and

<u>IT OPENED</u>!!! GOD, DIVINE MOTHER, TOUCHED MY HEART!!!

I felt such power! I am a *Bhakti* yogi at heart, and devotion to God is such a strong force. I cried, wept with such joy! I left class, went up to my room, lay on the bed in a fetal position, and wept more – sobs, intense sobs enveloping my entire body.

Later, when I returned to the class room, one of the instructors approached me. She said that she had been observing me while I chanted. She reported seeing a glow, radiance, develop around me. Responding, I told her I had no doubt that the glow appeared when Divine Mother entered my heart. The instructor said only one word, "Marvelous!" and walked away.

A second instructor came up to me and sat with me during a break. She thought my tears were from back pain. When I told her I had such a WONDERFUL heart opening, she said, "Oh yes, you come from that (Yogananda's) spiritual tradition."

I realized that she was correct – I did come from Yogananda's spiritual tradition. For years Roy Eugene Davis had spoken lovingly of his "Master," Paramahansa Yogananda. Roy's love was contagious. Living close to Roy Eugene Davis' Center for Spiritual Awareness had such a powerful impact upon my spiritual development. I felt very lucky and knew that I owed Roy such a great debt!

When it was time for meditation, I began walking to LOTUS. On the way, I wept. As I sobbed, I remembered that this was the same trail I stumbled on after I had such a powerful experience with Gurudev Swami Satchidananda three years earlier. I had not wept like that in the intervening three years. I later felt completely drained, but also completely peaceful.

Reproachfulness By July 1, one week after teacher training started, I was lying down in great pain with a muscle spasm. I reproached myself, "What am I doing here?!? How could I forget this terrible pain in just three years? I wanted to be of service to others and now I'm stuck ten hours away from home with a bad back!"

Every time I came to Yogaville, I realized just how insignificant my spiritual growth was, just how little I had realized my potential growth. It was very humbling.

The previous evening I had placed my forehead on the Swami Satchidananda's feet. At Roy Eugene Davis' request, I passed on Roy's greetings. "Give him my love" was Swami Satchidananda's response. Both Roy Eugene Davis and Swami

Satchidananda had my heart, which was quite wonderful, actually!

I Failed!!! I failed, FAILED, my qualifying exam for Intermediate Yoga Teacher Training. Several of the students believed <u>no</u> one failed. During the qualifying exam, I must have done a pretty miserable job. It was another humiliation. God must <u>really</u> love me – rubbing, scrubbing me into a wonderful diamond from a lump of coal.

I remained convinced that Divine Mother wanted me to go to Yogaville, that it was <u>not</u> a selfish desire but rather a desire to be of service to others. The previous spring, when a yoga class series ended, one of my students had pleaded, "This has become the most important part of my week. Can't we continue our yoga class?"

And I kept her image, her face, in my mind's eye during those two weeks of Intermediate Hatha Yoga Teacher Training. That image was such a comfort, and an inspiration. As a result of my training, I felt that I now had something to offer yoga students on an ongoing basis. I also had areas I could work on in my own practice.

When I returned home, I received a letter of encouragement from Swami Karunananda, one of my teachers:

25 July 2000

Dear Emerson,

Hari Om! All Love and Peace to you.

I was sorry that you left TT so abruptly, and I never had an opportunity to say goodbye and wish you well. Please let me know if I can be of any further service to you on your journey.

There's a reason for everything – a Higher Purpose behind all that transpires – no matter how random, undeserved or senseless things may seem. Have that faith and keep on going. Whatever lessons or meaning there may be will certainly make themselves known in time. In the meantime, be courageous, trusting, and joyful and let God take you where He will. There are no mistakes – only opportunities for our souls to grow and evolve and ultimately be free.

Trust in His love for you and enjoy the adventure.

Be well. Sending you loving prayers.

Om Shanti,

Karunananda

Consultation with Dr. Jack Woodard

On September 21, 2000 I went to see Dr. Jack Woodard. The following is a transcribed summary of that consultation:

Dr. Brooking: I was real intrigued when my gut started acting up when I left my position as professor. I couldn't believe that, with the meditation practice that I have and the spiritual practices that I do, my gut would immediately act up to some event – that this psychological – physical connection would be that strong. As usual, it is very humbling to me when I don't have control.

I've always been so externally motivated – you have to get to a job; you have certain responsibilities – that sort of thing. My whole life I've been more externally motivated than internally motivated, and boy, in my situation right now, if I'm not internally motivated, nothing happens. It takes a level of maturity and discipline that I'm hard pressed to come up with sometimes.

(I then describe how the president has destroyed me.)

Dr. Woodard: Emerson, it's an invitation to move up to the next level. Emerson, I've got some news for you, my friend – the president hasn't touched you. He can't reach you. He has destroyed a particular employment that you had, but he hasn't even touched you.

I think you've had a vivid demonstration of the hard wiring there is between the brain and the gut. They respond to the same neurotransmitters. They talk to each other all the time through the neurotransmitters.

Let me feel your pulse for a minute. ... The dynamics of your chi are good. Your yoga and your meditation practice are serving you well. It's better than money in the bank! The pulse is exactly the same as it was on 17 December, '96 – 68 beats a minute. That is another tribute to the power of your meditative practice. You're maintaining beautiful homeodynamics.

Emerson, I think the day will come when you will send the president a thank you note. The interesting thing about mission fulfillment and where you are in this crisis is that there is no way that mission fulfillment can be forced on you from the outside.

You can be stimulated, forced, coerced, encouraged, and prodded to do things that are useful things by outside sources. However, they cannot motivate you to fulfill the mission for which you came into this life. That has to come from within. That is part of the gift in this pain and crisis and fear and struggle that you're going through right now.

The other part is an AWESOMELY great opportunity for ego attrition. When you forgive – totally forgive – the president, you will have done a job of ego attrition that will empower you. It will empower you to back your ego out of the way enough to allow this flow of creative, healing energy to come through your energy system. Then this energy will flow to the people that it longs to go to in a way that will dumbfound and thrill you – the power with which that flow will take place when it's not obstructed by ego.

The other side of the "humbling" coin is empowerment. Anything that humbles us empowers us. Your ego is in the process of making a transition from master to servant, and it does not appreciate that one damn bit. You are now operating on a deeper level, and deeper means more power, more fulfillment, more joy.

Emerson, you are on the threshold of making a great enhancement of your quality of life!

(Immediately after our meeting, I was not satisfied with what Jack had prophesized. Yet, within a few years, everything he said turned out to be true. My catastrophic loss had resulted in a great enhancement of my quality of life.)

Stress Management Teacher Training

I Passed!!! From June 1 – 14, 2001, I returned to Yogaville for Stress Management Teacher Training. I arrived a day early so that I could take the qualifying exam in Intermediate Hatha Yoga. Since failing the exam the previous year, I had practiced teaching Intermediate Hatha Yoga to several students. With a year's practice, I had no trouble passing the qualifying exam.

I spent two weeks learning how to incorporate yoga philosophy and practice into a stress management class, and never use the word "yoga." It was a very worthwhile experience.

Stress Management classes were no longer painful events. I brought a reclining chair with me to Yogaville, which kept my spine from being overly stressed. I did not join the group for hatha, but did my own private hatha practice. Several times I visited a hot tub, which also helped my back. During the two weeks of training, I actually suffered very little and experienced almost no pain.

Hans Selye, M.D. defined stress as "A non-specific response of the body to any demand made upon it. It is immaterial whether the agent or situation we face is pleasant or unpleasant; all that counts is the intensity of the demand for readjustment or adaptation." During class, we discussed the stress cycle at length.

Stress Cycle

SELF/ME → EVENT → PERCEPTION → INTERPRETATION → EMOTION → BREATH CHANGE → PHYSICAL RESPONSE → BEHAVIOR

The earlier in the stress cycle one intervenes, the more effective the intervention. However, being able to successfully intervene is more difficult earlier (Interpretation) in the stress cycle than later (Breath Change).

Cognitive behavior therapy is quite difficult for some because it requires changing the belief system. Getting folks to change their interpretation of events is, therefore, not always easy. For example, I was being repeatedly told that losing my job had many positive aspects. Unfortunately, I just did not believe it then, and did not really believe it for a long time thereafter.

It is much easier to intervene in the stress cycle by changing one's breath. For instance, slow, deep breathing interrupts the stress cycle and makes it impossible to have anxiety attacks.

Yoga and Toccoa, Georgia

On Tuesday, September 11, 2001, I was scheduled to teach my first yoga class in Toccoa, Georgia. I was so excited because, as far as I knew, this was the first yoga class offered in Toccoa in eleven years!

Though I had great difficulty finding a location in which to hold my class, I was eventually offered a very nice church setting. The Toccoa recreation department was certainly not excited about the opportunity to host my class, and I knew why. Eleven years earlier, I had incredulously followed the hoopla created by some Toccoa townspeople that generated headlines worldwide.

Eleven years earlier, the recreation department had sponsored a yoga class series titled "Take Time to Relax". The teacher was to be Carolyn Davis. (Carolyn led the Sunday meditations at the Center for Spiritual Awareness when I first began attending in 1989. She was a sincere truth seeker and I had great love and respect for her.)

One man spearheaded a movement to have the class canceled. He declared that people who relax their minds by performing yoga are opening the door to the devil. "The people who are signed up for the class are just walking into it like cattle to a slaughter. Half of yoga is a branch of Eastern mysticism, and it has strong occult influences." (*Toccoa Record*, September 6, 1990)

Citizens from several churches, including Baptist, Lutheran, and Church of God, complained to local officials. No public meeting was held, but instead officials discussed the issue on the telephone. Bowing to pressure from the protesters, a majority of city and county commissioners agreed to the cancellation of the yoga class.

What no one in Toccoa could have anticipated was the public outcry over the decision. Not only did local citizens, including the twenty-six people who had signed up for the class, express outrage, but also people from many other places. CNN and the BBC picked up the story and broadcasted it around the world. Letters from as far away as China came pouring into Toccoa. The mayor even had a live interview with a radio station in San Francisco. The general sentiment expressed was well summed up in the following letter:

Mayor,
Toccoa, Georgia
September 8, 1990
Dear Mayor,
This is a simple thank you note for bringing resounding laughter into a too-serious world.

A two column story hit our local paper about the Pharisee in your midst who succeeded in canceling a yoga class. Jesus laughed at them, too. We have such clowns here, as well. A lot of good Christians here are still chuckling. Thanks again. Watsonville, California 95076

When a public meeting was finally convened, around a hundred folks appeared. Some drove quite a ways to get there. Half wanted the recreation department to sponsor the yoga class; half did not. They came armed with Bibles, scholarly essays, dictionaries and encyclopedias. In the end, the commissioners upheld their decision not to allow the recreation department to sponsor the yoga class.

During the meeting, yoga was declared a religion. However, after discovering that public recreation facilities had been used by religious groups for years, commissioners agreed that they could not prevent a private group from renting the facilities to teach a yoga class. So the facility was rented and Carolyn Davis taught the class, with more than thirty attending.

A police car was positioned in front of the recreation department during the first class. The mayor also asked a "couple of big old bruisers" to attend. After the class, the mayor reported, "It's been very quiet. No sign of the Devil. I keep looking, but I don't see any horns. No one has grown a tail, either." [Nadis, S. (1992, May). Yoga Wars. *Omni, 14(8),* 80]

Many Toccoa citizens were embarrassed by the uproar – many others were quite pleased. As the man who started it all stated, "Yoga is a branch of the occult. These abilities that you get from yoga are demonically inspired. God help you if you take it. I'm glad it all came out. God has awakened Christians to the encroaching of the occult. Our whole purpose was to alert the nation to what was happening." (*Anderson Independent*, September 11, 1990)

Both sides of the issue claimed victory. However, the mayor of Toccoa declared that no one had won. "We're all losers because it divides the community." The mayor added, "And also, the image of Toccoa has been tarnished. Most of the criticism in the letters weren't necessarily criticizing yoga, but criticizing the city of Toccoa for not allowing the program."

I wanted to include this story of yoga and Toccoa, Georgia, because it epitomizes the strong influence of Southern Christian fundamentalism in this area of the world. This part of the country is the area of my birth, the area I call home. I know Christian fundamentalism well, as I was reared in it. Even today, it exerts a powerful influence.

For example, when I was teaching at my four year, liberal arts college, I had students declare that God never intended Christians to be happy. Another belief expressed was that, if Christians relaxed their minds, the devil would jump in and take over. As the director of the School of Bible and Theology at a nearby college stated, "If yoga has gotten a person in trouble, that person would have to renounce it frequently and break his bondage with Satan. He'd then need to fill that area with God's spirit – hopefully the Lord Jesus Christ." [Nadis, S. (1992, May). Yoga Wars. *Omni, 14(8),* 80]

You may believe that yoga is a common, widely accepted practice. However, in this geographic area, that is often not true. Even as late as 2005, when a yoga teacher moved to Toccoa, an attempt was made to keep classes out of town. At that time, yoga was described as "rotten" by the same element that had started the uproar in 1990.

So, when I taught my first yoga class in Toccoa, Georgia, on September 11, 2001, it was the first class to be offered there in eleven years. That evening, I was pleasantly surprised to find twenty-six students eager to learn and practice. And each time I taught a class in Toccoa, I dedicated the class to Carolyn Davis, Toccoa's yoga pioneer.

September 11, 2001

Tuesday morning, September 11th, I was enjoying some "God Time" in my center, doing my yoga practice. A man, who was suffering from anxiety attacks, called to cancel his morning appointment. He stated that he was too upset to relax. "Have you heard the news? Two planes have hit the World Trade Towers in New York and one has hit the Pentagon."

I urged the man to use his relaxation skills to help maintain his balance during this emergency. His response was not encouraging. I was reminded of one of the men I worked with at the addiction treatment center. One day, he learned that a warrant had been issued for his arrest. When I asked him if he used his relaxation skills to help him maintain his balance, he was incredulous and exclaimed, "Surely you don't expect me to relax when I am upset!"

I explained to both of these men that, if they could not use relaxation skills when they were upset, why bother to learn them? What good were they? The men were just wasting their time.

After I heard about the attacks, I walked down to the house and, in tears, gathered my wife and son together. I apologized for the sorry state of the world. I then turned on TV and we watched together. The World Trade Towers had fallen and there was much fear, death, and destruction. This was so painful to watch on television!

I was teary-eyed several times that week. The stock exchange closed all week and the whole nation was very tense and nervous. The first war of the 21st century had been declared. Much uncertainty lay ahead.

I was so thankful and joyous to be at Panther Brook. I had enjoyed my home for fifteen years and that had been a priceless gift. The peace of my "God Time" was such a contrast to the fear and hatred in the outside world. I was so thankful for my peaceful environment. It provided such a wonderful place for creating and for living in the moment, the golden present moment.

Meher Baba's Spiritual Center

During a conversation with Robert Wootton, he suggested that I might enjoy visiting Meher Spiritual Center in Myrtle Beach, South Carolina. Robert's suggestions carried a lot of weight, as he was the one who suggested I visit Southern Dharma Retreat Center. Certainly visiting Southern Dharma turned out to be a winner of an idea!

So from May 31 to June 5, 2002, I visited Meher Spiritual Center. It encompasses five hundred pristine acres, located on the beach. The Center is dedicated to Avatar Meher Baba, who visited the center in 1952, 1956, and 1958, and declared it his "Home in the West."

Baba maintained Silence from July 10, 1925 until the end of his life on January 31, 1969. He explained his Silence by stating, "Because man has been deaf to the principles and precepts laid down by God in the past, in this Avataric Form I observe Silence. You have asked for and been given enough words – it is now time to live them."

While at the Center, I felt my mind and body getting calmer and calmer. While sitting in the Library, with its view over the lake and beach beyond, I spent hours reading about Meher Baba and watching movies of his life. Later, I rode in an authentic gondola, made in Venice, Italy, and purchased at the Chicago World's Fair.

I took a small row boat out onto the mile-long, fresh water lake and saw <u>many</u> fish, some quite large. I also saw two large snakes and two alligators, one small and one large. Several shore birds added to the beauty.

I spent my mornings and evenings on the beach chanting and meditating – <u>very</u> nice! Hikes along the undeveloped shoreline were also special. It was a <u>wonderful</u> beach experience!

I felt <u>very</u> relaxed, having enjoyed hours of meditation/prayer. I visited Meher Baba's home, the "Meher Abode." His bedroom proved to be a <u>very</u> powerful experience. It was an air conditioned home but I began sweating profusely. I knelt beside his bed and gently placed my forehead on his bed. It was a beautiful, moving moment.

I planned to return to the Meyer Spiritual Center. Certainly, it was a jewel, a unique beach experience!!!

The following is from "Meher Baba's Universal Message" (Published by Meher Spiritual Center, Inc., 10200 Highway 17 N., Myrtle Beach, South Carolina 29577. Kind permission to use quotes from *The Universal Message* by Meher Baba has been granted by the copyright holder, Avatar Meher Baba Perpetual Public Charitable Trust, Ahmednagar, India.):

The Seven Realities Meher Baba gives no importance to creed, dogma, caste systems, and the performance of religious ceremonies and rites, but to the UNDERSTANDING of the following seven Realities:

1. The only REAL EXISTENCE is that of the One and only God, who is the Self in every (finite) self.

2. The only REAL LOVE is the Love for this Infinity (God), which arouses an intense longing to see, know, and become one with its Truth (God).

3. The only REAL SACRIFICE is that in which, in pursuance of this Love, all things, body, mind, position, welfare, and even life itself are sacrificed.

4. The only REAL RENUNICATION is that which abandons, even in the midst of worldly duties, all selfish thoughts and desires.

5. The only REAL KNOWLEDGE is the Knowledge that God is the inner dweller in good people and so-called bad, in saint and so-called sinner. This Knowledge requires you to help all equally as circumstances demand, without expectation of reward, and when compelled to take part in a dispute, to act without the slightest trace of enmity or hatred; to try to make others happy with brotherly or sisterly feeling for each one; to harm no one in thought, word, or deed, not even those who harm you.

6. The only REAL CONTROL is the discipline of the senses from indulgence in low desires, which alone ensures absolute purity of character.

7. The only REAL SURRENDER is that in which the poise is undisturbed by any adverse circumstance, and the individual, amidst every kind of hardship, is resigned with perfect calm to the will of God.

Baba's ministry is well summarized in the following quote:

"Trust God completely and He will solve all difficulties. Faithfully leave everything to Him and He will see to everything. Love God sincerely and He will reveal Himself. And as you love, your heart must love so that even your mind is not aware of it. As you love God whole-heartedly and honestly, sacrificing everything at the altar of this supreme love, you will realize the Beloved within you."

More about Meher Baba and the Meher Spiritual Center can be found at www.mehercenter.org

Being Lived by the Tao

Attending a four-day Taoist retreat (September 25 – 28, 2003) at Southern Dharma led by Linda Gooding, was marvelous. Linda titled the retreat "Being Lived by the Tao. She had been a student of Taoism for many years and taught weekly meditation classes in the Atlanta area. Her approach to teaching meditation combined her own personal experience and understanding with the practical perspective that came from many years as a biomedical scientist and teacher.

During the retreat I moved energy throughout the body and did two sweats in the sweat lodge. The retreat left me feeling quite WONDERFUL! I also felt that it set the stage for the "*Kundalini* Crisis" which followed.

"Kundalini Crisis"

The next weekend (October 3 – 5) I attended a "Universal Chanting" retreat at Southern Dharma. The retreat was led by Jon Seskevich and Mark Smith. In 1975, Jon started his training as a teacher of meditation and healing under the mentorship of meditation expert, psychologist, spiritual teacher and writer, Ram Dass (Richard Alpert, Ph.D.). Jon had extensive experience in devotional chanting. Mark Smith was a singer/songwriter. (Adapted from SDRC 2003 Brochure.)

Chanting opened my heart in a profound way, and, coming immediately after the Taoist retreat where much energy was created, set the stage for the "*Kundalini* Crisis" which emerged. For hours we would chant and meditate, chant and meditate. I found the schedule to be extremely intense and powerful. My heart seemed more open than ever before.

On October 3rd, I had a dream, which I titled "Destroying the Ego":

Dream: I am supposed to be in one group but I am in another. The group I am supposed to be in is known as the "health" group. While I was in the first group my index finger of my right hand became infected with something in it. When I return to the "health group", the "health" group rips apart my index finger, shredding it to the bone. I pass out from the pain and roll around in the dirt. Two people from the "health" group cradle me in their arms and clean my wound.

Interpretation: In yoga philosophy, the index finger represents the ego. My ego must be shredded to be fully in the "health" group.

The next day, the "*Kundalini* Crisis" began. That morning I continued to alternate between periods of meditating and singing God's praise. Saturday afternoon, during a break, I walked to the knoll and lay in a hammock. As I swung back and forth, I noticed the following symptoms: headaches, total exhaustion, dizziness, and generally feeling unwell. It felt as though my soul would not completely come back into my body.

Being a true Lover of God, I continued this intensive practice of chanting and meditating, chanting and meditating, until the retreat ended on Sunday. Unfortunately, my symptoms also continued.

Sunday afternoon, when I tried to leave Southern Dharma, my departure met with disaster. As I backed over a bridge, I could clearly see the road in my rear view window. But, in a flash. I was bursting through a rock wall, leaving more than thirty per cent of my camper hanging over empty space above the creek. There was a clear danger that the camper would actually turn over into the creek!

Thank God there were a couple of people around who figured out how to save the day. When I started to remove a rock that was denting the camper, they stopped me and pointed out that the rock was the only thing stopping the camper from turning over and plunging into the creek. They then engineered more supports and I was able to successfully drive back onto the bridge.

On the way home I stopped four times to eat everything I could find that was heavy and greasy – fried chicken, eggs, candy bars, and popcorn – just trying to stay grounded enough to drive. When I arrived home, I avoided driving for weeks. I just did not feel safe behind the steering wheel of a car.

This was another reminder that these spiritual practices were really quite powerful. I searched the internet for "*Kundalini* Crisis" and was amazed at what I read. Many poor souls reported life shattering *Kundalini* experiences. Some reported never recovering from them.

It was humorously ironic that, just prior to the chanting retreat, I had been thinking how stale my spiritual life was becoming – just following the same routines. In the middle of my "*Kundalini* Crisis," my previous spiritual practices no longer looked so dull, and I longed for a return to "dullness." I felt so uncertain about my future that I made sure my will was in good order and my burial instructions were complete.

I was desperate to get help and spoke to several people about the state I was in. My soul just did not seem to want to completely return to my body. Some comments made about my condition included the following:

John Orr: "The *kundalini* energy is rising and being stuck, blocked in your head. The cure is to move it back down to your second chakra. Come to my retreat and we'll work on it."

(As much as I wanted to, I did not go to John's retreat. I was afraid to drive. I just did not feel together enough for such a trip.)

Linda Gooding: "You're not shattered, but rather more disjointed. You need to breathe consciously into your *Tan-T'ien* (Umbilicus) to move the energy from your head to your *Tan-T'ien*."

New Age Friend: "You're shattered. Part of you doesn't want to return to your body. Your soul experienced such bliss it doesn't want to return. The cure is to go into deep meditation and ask your beloveds to help you come back into your body."

My brother visited. During his visit, he noted that this was the first time in my life that my ego had not been in the way. This was why I had such a forceful experience. In my dream, which occurred the night before this experience began, my ego was destroyed. The index finger represented the ego – stripped to the bone.

On Sunday, my brother and I went to CSA for meditation. I met with Roy Eugene Davis for a couple of minutes after the meditation and described my experience, my *"Kundalini* Crisis." Roy said he had never had such an experience and offered these encouraging words: "Hang in there and see if it doesn't get better."

While at CSA, I also told Marty Wuttke, who taught brain wave biofeedback, about my condition and asked him for suggestions. He demonstrated some exercises that stimulated the microcosmic orbit of Taoism. He said it was blocked energy causing my discomfort. (Pain is interpreted as blocked energy in Taoist philosophy.)

On Monday, I spoke with a New Age couple by telephone. I gave permission for the wife to contact my higher self. The wife went into trance and contacted my higher self to find out why the pain had not gone away. She called me back to say that she was told that my work here on earth was done. I had achieved my purpose for this incarnation and my spirit wanted to move on and leave this body. I had to decide if I was going to die and leave this body or stay and reenter my body fully. I had not fully made that decision.

When I asked the wife what my purpose was that had been fulfilled, she said I worked with many students and introduced them to ideas and practices they may not have otherwise been exposed to. I had also fathered my son, and he was a great soul with a great destiny. What I taught him would always be with him.

I spoke to a board member of Southern Dharma and described my situation. When I relayed my dream of how my index finger was stripped to the bone, he pointed out that shamans report dreams of having all their flesh torn off as part of their initiation into shamanic powers.

While I was having all these conversations, I was not sure what to believe. I did know that I was fascinated, very fascinated!

By October 23rd, my "*Kundalini* Crisis" seemed to be calming down a great deal. I still felt dizzy at times but my head did not burn all the time and I did not have <u>nearly</u> as many headaches.

My meditations were not as deep as they had been in the height of the "Kundalini Crisis." When it began, I would close my eyes to meditate and immediately flow into dark emptiness. As the "Kundalini Crisis" slowly abated, my "monkey mind" slowly returned.

Prior to the "*Kundalini* Crisis," in my longer, more intense meditations, I had fleetingly experienced this dark emptiness. But never before had I been able to flow directly into dark emptiness with such ease. Dark emptiness was not an uncomfortable place, but to rest in that state for long periods was new and unusual.

I called Dr. Amrita McLanahan at Yogaville and described my symptoms. She said the symptoms resembled those that occur with a constricted blood flow to the brain and suggested I see a chiropractor for an adjustment. I immediately had my chiropractor give me an adjustment, and most of my remaining symptoms disappeared. Glory Be!!!

For the first time in weeks, I felt like I might actually survive this "*Kundalini* Crisis"! As I later considered what had transpired, I was struck by the levels of interpretation, the levels of analysis, which are possible when explaining the same phenomenon. I did not feel that any of the people I consulted were "right" or "wrong." Instead, many were operating on different levels, with dissimilar philosophies.

Perhaps I never had a "*Kundalini* Crisis." Perhaps my experience could be adequately explained using a physiological level of analysis – constricted blood flow to the brain. And yet does that do justice to the phenomenon? On a spiritual level, the experience shook me to my core.

My ego, like my index finger in the dream, had been thoroughly shredded. If the physiological level of analysis was totally adequate, how could it explain that powerful dream that occurred the night **before the symptoms began?**

Regardless of the wide range of possible physical/spiritual interpretations and explanations available (from kind and caring people), this was a powerful experience for me. It left me with new appreciation of the power of my spiritual practices.

A Note from my Abbot and Teacher

In March, 2004, I joyously received a note from Phra. Khru Khantayaporn, my abbot and teacher in Thailand. He was now eighty-five years old.

March, 2004

Hello! How are you, Dr. E. Brooking?

Is the Buddha image which I gave you in 1985 still remaining? Moreover, how about the meditation that I taught you? You have told me about it; that it is a kind of happiness which occurs in your mind. How about this feeling?

Now, I'm not staying at Wat Srikerd. I moved to stay at cemetery "Trilak" in Mae Wang District. I stay there for 10 years. If you would like to contact me, you could contact me at Wat Srikerd.

Grant happiness

It was a sweet experience learning a little more about the abbot's life since we were together nineteen years earlier. Periodically, over the years, I had communicated with him and Phra. Songdej, always sending them donations. But I had never received a letter from the abbot. Speaking different languages continued to be a hurdle.

I quickly responded to the abbot's letter. I briefly described my current meditation practices and assured him that the Buddha image he gave me in 1985 was on my private altar. I also added a donation.

Once again I thanked the abbot for the many kindnesses he had shown me in 1985. I acknowledged the great debt that I owed him. The Serenity Meditation he so lovingly taught me had a profound impact on my spiritual life. Indeed, my meditation practice changed the course of my life in very positive ways. The peace and joy it brought into my life were precious jewels I treasured always.

Meher Spiritual Center – My Second Spiritual Hospital

Over the years, I did several ten-day meditation retreats at Meher Spiritual Center. Once again, meditation/prayer, silence, solitude, and fasting facilitated the renewal of my spiritual life. During each retreat, I regained some balance and sanity in my life. My times at the ashram were so healing!!!

Meher Spiritual Center had become my second great spiritual hospital – a powerful place for rest, meditation/prayer, and the renewal of my spiritual life. My first spiritual hospital had been Southern Dharma Retreat Center.

My retreats at Southern Dharma afforded me the opportunity to learn about many spiritual traditions, and to actually practice those traditions. As the years passed, I felt capable and secure in selecting those spiritual practices that I found most useful. I knew that I would always feel grateful to Southern Dharma and the powerful influences it had in my spiritual life. But I no longer felt a need to learn and experience a variety of spiritual practices. Instead, I needed a place to translate what I had learned into intensive practice. Meher Spiritual Center fulfilled that need.

In <u>so</u> many ways I felt like I had entered heaven – the lake I overlooked was filled with fish and alligators. Belted kingfishers, herons, egrets, and ospreys were common sights. Beyond the lake there were sand dunes and further on the Atlantic Ocean, stretching blue and endless beyond the trees. And, of course, there was the unrelenting pounding of the surf.

Baba's abode sat close to my cabin. Whenever his abode was open, I meditated/prayed in his bedroom. Baba's small bedroom was the most powerful, sacred meditation space I had ever embraced.

For decades "Baba Lovers" had worshiped around his bed, and their energy and his energy combined to create a transforming presence, drawing me into superconscious states and filling me with love. Baba once stated, "I am the ocean of love. Fear me not but love me more and more." That, I feel, is God's message to all of us.

Emptiness – Meditation in Baba's Bedroom On September 15, 2006, I experienced a most profound encounter. That morning I did my yoga as the sun rose, ate a small breakfast, walked a four mile circle down the beach and through the woods, and then visited the Meher Abode.

While in Baba's bedroom, I seemed to melt into a dark place, dark emptiness filled with peace, transcending all else. My body seemed literally to turn to goo, melt and dissolve, leaving my mind to roam free until it too melted away, leaving only dark, benign emptiness....

Emptiness!

I do not think I was in that state long, but it was profound! The silence of that experience and days of silence at Meyer Spiritual Center continue to stay with me. I often feel quite content to just rest in the silence, listening to the sacred inner sound, the great OM, the sound of God who is always with me.

Even now, however, I find myself yearning for more. "I am the bubble – make me the sea!" Only by God's grace can becoming the sea occur. Having once been intoxicated in Divine Bliss, I cry, "**Again, Again!!!**"

For hours I sit by the ocean, waves caressing my feet, and chant and meditate. My favorite chant by the sea is written by Paramahansa Yogananda. It is titled, "I Am the Bubble, Make Me the Sea." [Yogananda, P. (1974). *Cosmic chants*. Los Angeles, CA: Self-Realization Fellowship. p. 45]

At times, I chant out loud, sometimes loudly, sometimes softly. During other periods, I chant only within my heart. I seem to be able to chant for hours without becoming tired or bored. Perhaps that is because I meditate for long periods between chanting. Or perhaps it is the sound of the birds and the ocean waves, the feel of the sand beneath my feet and between my toes, the beach smells or the taste of salt spray on my lips. Certainly never knowing when a particularly large wave will inundate me helps me stay alert, and gives me such joy! Especially since I mostly keep my eyes closed!

Spiritual Advancement During retreats at my spiritual hospital (a.k.a. Meher Spiritual Center), each day I move deeper and deeper into superconsciousness!

I am reminded of what Sri Yukteswar (Yogananda's guru) said to Paramhansa Yogananda about true spiritual advancement:

> Paramhansa Yogananda: "I want to know sir - when shall I find God?"
>
> Sri Yukteswar: "You have already found Him."
>
> Paramhansa Yogananda: "O no, sir, I don't think so!"
>
> Sri Yukteswar: (My guru was smiling.) "I am sure you aren't expecting a venerable Personage, adorning a throne in some antiseptic corner of the cosmos! I see,

however, that you are imagining that the possession of miraculous powers is knowledge of God. One might have the whole universe, and find the Lord elusive still! Spiritual advancement is not measured by one's outward powers, but only by the depth of his bliss in meditation.

Ever-new Joy is God. He is inexhaustible; as you continue your meditations during the years, He will beguile you with an infinite ingenuity. Devotees like yourself who have found the way to God never dream of exchanging Him for any other happiness; He is seductive beyond thought of competition.

How quickly we weary of earthly pleasures! Desire for material things is endless; man is never satisfied completely, and pursues one goal after another. The 'something else' he seeks is the Lord, who alone can grant lasting joy.

Outward longings drive us from the Eden within; they offer false pleasures which only impersonate soul-happiness. The lost paradise is quickly gained through divine meditation.

As God is unanticipatory Ever-Newness, we never tire of Him. Can we be surfeited with bliss, delightfully varied throughout eternity?.... meditation furnishes a twofold proof of God. Ever-new joy is evidence of His existence, convincing to our very atoms.

Also, in meditation one finds His instant guidance, His adequate response to every difficulty." (*Autobiography of a Yogi*, Paramhansa Yogananda, 1946, pp.148-149.)

Roy Eugene Davis often speaks of how Yogananda would challenge his disciples by urging that every day they meditate more deeply than they had the day before. I feel this is a wonderful goal, but I rarely can claim that the depth of my bliss in meditation increases daily. However, during my retreats at

Meher Spiritual Center, I succeed in meeting Yogananda's challenge. My bliss increases and deepens daily!

Legacy

On September 26, 2006, a friend told me a most wonderful story. All of the classroom teachers in her school were feeling enormous stress. One of the special education teachers confessed that she would be in a state of collapse from all the stress except for the fact that, while a student at the local college, she had taken a course with a teacher, Dr. Brooking. He taught her techniques to use to handle her stress.

As a student, she was young and did not think she would ever need to use stress management techniques. Now they were her life saver. When my friend told me the special education teacher's name, I did not remember her. But the story made my heart leap for joy and reminded me that my years of service at the college were not wasted, were not meaningless.

This was true primary prevention of mental health problems. The stress management techniques I taught her sustained her in high stress situations and kept her from collapse. I was proud to have dedicated my life to these kinds of activities, happy that this was part of my legacy.

Teacher Training at Center for Spiritual Awareness

During September, 2008, Roy Eugene Davis conducted a week-long teacher training program at CSA. Roy's training was a powerful way to enhance my own ministry!

I so enjoyed living in my own private ashram, Panther Brook, but I recognized that I had "a calling to spread the good news" that was lifelong. During his talks, Roy emphasized that he felt it was important to "have a calling to teach Kriya Yoga."

When Teacher Training ended, I saw Roy going to his car. I thanked him again for letting me participate and shared with him how special the week was for me. As he spoke, he tapped me three times on the chest at the heart center. I felt a surge of energy there and for the next five days felt <u>very</u> unsettled. I was completely discombobulated!!!

I just could not seem to focus, to be settled. I did not fully realize just how powerful the experience with Roy was until Tuesday night as I tried to sleep. The inner sound was **_SO LOUD_** that it was a roar in my head and I could not sleep.

Once again, I could not handle these energy surges, either emotionally or physically. If God ever did come into my heart and stay there, I suppose I would burn out, pop like a light bulb!

When I saw Roy the next Sunday before meditation, I told him of my experiences, and how I could not sleep Tuesday night. He said one word – "*Shakti.*" When I asked him if he intended *shakti-pot*, the passing of divine energy to me, he said, "Sometimes it just happens."

He started to walk into the meditation hall, but then turned and tapped me again on the heart, saying with a grin, "You won't be able to sleep tonight either!" My wife, who was in front of him, said that, when he walked into the meditation hall, he was laughing merrily. I so enjoy having a playful guru!

Since I first met Roy in 1988, this was the second time that I had felt the transfer of *shakti* from him. The other time occurred during a Kriya Yoga initiation, when he placed one hand at my third eye and the other on my heart. I felt a jolt that time, for sure!!!

Roy continued to have a strong influence on my spiritual growth and I was thankful for his presence in my life.

Living my Dream

In February, 2010, I received the following e-mail that filled me with such joy:

Hello Dr. Brooking!

I took a Stress Management Class from you years ago. It was your last year at the college and the best class I ever took. I found you by looking at your ad for free yoga classes. I would like to make reservations for yoga and also for meditation. I hope there are some spots open! Please let me know what I need to do to get started.

Your class was the best class I ever took. I'll never forget going into a deep meditative state in your class. It hasn't happened since so I'm really looking forward to your classes being open. I also remember you talking of having silent retreats. It looks like to me you have been able to live out your dream!

I'm a massage therapist now! I love what I do but I need to work on myself more.

Thanks and I hope to hear from you soon.

"It looks like to me you have been able to live out your dream!" I felt that was true! The e-mail reminded me that my work had a positive impact on many lives, which was quite a comforting thought!

Driving While God Intoxicated

In July (twelve days) and September (eight days), 2010, I visited Meher Spiritual Center, my spiritual hospital. I brought enough food and other supplies with me so that leaving the ashram was not necessary for several days. Extended periods within the ashram intensified my meditative experience.

I experienced some deep meditations in Baba's bedroom, on the porch of my cabin, and the beach. A few meditations in Baba's bedroom lasted over an hour! If my spine were in better shape, I would do one hour meditations all the time. Generally, the longer I sit, the deeper I go!

One afternoon, as I was driving over to the beach access within the ashram, a deer darted in front of my car. I continued to watch it as it merrily wandered on down a trail. I was totally transfixed by its beauty, its grace. Only one thing was wrong with my enthusiasm with the deer – I neglected to apply the brakes. It was at this point that I hit the tree!

My driver's side view mirror slammed against my window, shattering the mirror.   I was very lucky the window did not also break! I had to spend part of the next two days having the mirror replaced. I most regretted having to leave the ashram and make two trips across Myrtle Beach. Myrtle Beach has a LOT OF CONCRETE, a LOT OF BUILDINGS, and a LOT OF PEOPLE!!! Meher Spiritual Center does not have a lot of any of these. It only has a LOT OF PEACE!

This was a good wake-up call, reminding me to be mindful. I really should not be behind the wheel of a car when I am that full of God, when Divine Mother fills me with such rapture. If an accident did occur, I am thankful there is no test the police can give me to determine if I have too much God in me, that I am over the "legal" limit of God Intoxication.

Roy Eugene Davis Authorizes Teaching Kriya Yoga

Roy Eugene Davis authorized me to teach Kriya Yoga, including Kriya Pranayama, on January 2, 2011. I wanted to teach this meditation technique to my students, but did not do so. I felt I needed Roy's authorization.

We were about to begin Sunday morning meditation, and I asked, "Will you authorize me to teach Kriya Yoga?" He responded, "You do it – teach it!" and tapped me on my chest, over my heart. I can, even now, feel the warmth of that touch.

I added, "I find it a very useful meditation technique, but I did not want to teach it until I had your authorization." Roy replied, "You know how to teach it. Teach it!"

Later, over lunch, I relayed this story to some friends. They toasted me in congratulations! After lunch, I was in the grocery store. One of the lunch group came up to me and emphasized, "This is **HUGE**!!!"

I am pleased to be able to share Kriya Yoga, including Kriya Pranayama, with others. May I prove myself worthy of such an honor!

Benefits of Meditation

Experience teaches me that Roy Eugene Davis is correct in his description of the benefits of meditation. Regularly meditating to a level of superconsciousness allows the innate purity of my essence of being to purify my mind and illumine my consciousness. Such meditation results in the following benefits:

1. Physical benefits: Stress reduction; relief from stress-related symptoms; slowing of biological aging processes; enhanced immune function; refinement of brain centers through which spiritual qualities can be more easily processed.

2. Psychological benefits: Increased ability to focus, concentrate, and think more rationally; increased ability to let go of distracting thoughts; increased peace of mind; respite from relentless mind-chatter; weakening of addictive tendencies, harmful habits, and troublesome subconscious conditionings.

3. Spiritual benefits: Experience of wholeness; increased compassion; clearing of outmoded thought patterns; increased intuition, insight, and creativity; increased ability to view events and circumstances with dispassionate objectivity; enlightenment (identification as Self instead of self).

Meditation Handbook Summary

Meditation is a **relaxed, focused, uninterrupted awareness**. In this book I have presented sufficient information for you to begin a new meditation practice or deepen an existing practice. I will now briefly review the information previously presented. Each term that is bold, italicized, and underlined can be found in the Table of Contents at the beginning of this book.

Relaxed Awareness
Meditation requires the ability to let go and let God. If you are unable to relax, deep meditation is unlikely.

Probably the easiest way to relax is to focus on belly breathing. The ***Diaphragmatic Breathing Exercise*** (p. 69) is a good introduction. If you are a chest breather and have difficulty breathing into your belly, lie in ***The Crocodile Posture*** (p. 64). This posture will teach you the appropriate muscles to use to breathe diaphragmatically.

When you are a proficient belly breather, then master Three Part Breathing (Deergha Swaasam) described by Swami Satchidananda in his article ***The Breath of Life*** (p. 111). When done correctly, you will actually be breathing in seven times more air than a normal breath.

Breathe in to the belly, then the chest, and finally the upper chest, so even your collar bones rise. Then breathe out in just the opposite manner, emptying the upper chest, the chest, and the belly. Draw in the belly at the end of the out breath to exhale all the air. And then begin again. Do not hold the breath at any point and do not strain. Breathe only through the nose.

The ***Introduction to Progressive Muscle Relaxation*** (p. 36) and ***Progressive Muscle Relaxation Instructions*** (p. 37) will provide you with a powerful entry into deep relaxation. Just remember to keep breathing full, deep breaths as you tighten and release the major muscle groups in your body.

During and at the end of your progressive muscle relaxation, do not forget to include some autogenic suggestions. *Introduction to Autogenic Training* (p. 74) and *Autogenic Training Instructions* (p. 75) will outline the procedure.

When you feel like you are totally relaxed and could not possibly relax any further, take you finger temperature. If it is not 95°s or higher, raise it. The autogenic suggestion, "My hand is warm and heavy" may help. Or take your GSR2 and lower the tone. See *Thermal Biofeedback* (p.60) and *Electrodermal Biofeedback* (p. 62).

If you would like to buy a GSR2, it will cost around seventy-five dollars at www.thoughttechnology.com If you mention this book, they will give you a ten percent discount.

Begin your meditation/prayer practice with *Alternate Nostril Breathing* (Naadi Suddhi, Nerve Purification) (p.71). [If your nose is congested, do a *Neti (Nasal) Wash* (p. 65) first.] Remember to do your Three Part Breathing (Deergha Swaasam) throughout your Alternate Nostril Breathing exercise. Focus on having the exhalation twice as long as the inhalation. If you breathe in to the count of three, breathe out to the count of six.

Over time, increase your breath until you can comfortably breathe in to the count of ten and out to the count of twenty. You can gain more control over your breath by using Ujjayi breathing. In Ujjayi breathing you constrict your throat, slightly closing the glottis, like you were trying to fog a mirror. Ujjayi breathing makes a slight sound and gives you more control over your inhalation and exhalation.

But always remember, when doing pranayamas, not to strain. Back off if you find yourself gasping for air. Because you are dealing with such delicate organs as the lungs, heart, and the nerve centers, take great care not to strain. I have heard that too much strain may lead to harm, such as a deranged mind and heart problems. Pranayamas are so powerful that many yoga teachers never teach them in beginning classes. So act responsibly!

In this book, I am not giving instructions on Kapalabhati (Skull Shining), Bhastrika (Bellows Breath), breath retention, or Bandhas (locks) as I feel it is wiser to learn these skills while directly supervised by a teacher (guru). They are wonderfully powerful tools for controlling the flow of prana and raising the latent Kundalini energy, but I believe they are best learned under supervision. However, if you cannot find a teacher (guru) to teach you these skills, please feel free to contact me.

Focused Awareness
In this book I have outlined several techniques to help focus and relax your mind. Teaching meditation to a lot of people over many years has taught me that, if you are open to practicing various meditation techniques, you will eventually find one that suits you well. There are hundreds from which to choose. However, the trick is to not jump around too fast, using lots of different techniques. You must use each one long enough to truly experience it. That is part of the art of discovering a useful meditation technique.

As my meditations deepened, I experienced a great deal of fear. I had to learn to "let go and let God." I spent many years building my ego, but success in meditation required that I let it go and merge in the infinite. It was my path to Self- and God-realization.

It is ironic that this struggle exists for most of us. You may experience it also. I discovered, and you may too, that there is no need for fear. This struggle is a paradox. The ego, the bubble, can become part of the sea, and yet will still be the bubble. The individual ego can survive, though transformed!

Of course, my "hook" into the meditation practice was the Serenity Meditation. *Introduction to Serenity Meditation* (p. 26) and *Serenity Meditation Instructions* (p. 27) describe the technique. If you do not have time for extensive meditation practice periods, then the Serenity Meditation may work for you.

You should be able to complete your meditation within twenty to thirty minutes.

If you would like, I would be pleased to initiate you into the Serenity Meditation. I only ask in return that you pledge to practice the Serenity Meditation for one month, at least once every day, for at least twenty minutes.

When you have longer periods of time for more intensive practice, I would recommend you practice Vipassana Meditation. *__Mindfulness (Vipassana) Meditation Instructions__* (p. 32) are written quite clearly and include someone you can contact if you have any questions. In this book, you have read how Vipassana Meditation opened parts in me that I did not know existed. Learning to deal successfully with these dark, unknown, frightening parts of my psyche helped me heal, to become more open and less afraid. My vipassana practice, and indeed all my meditation practices, served as Divine Psychotherapy.

Kriya Pranayama Meditation is a simple, but powerful, meditation technique. I have not described it in detail because that would be inappropriate. It is best taught by personal transmission. You should have a teacher (guru) personally initiate you in this practice. My guru, Roy Eugene Davis, has authorized me to initiate others, and I will be pleased to discuss this with you, if you desire.

Mantra meditation is another meditation technique you can use to focus your awareness. *__Learning to Elicit the Relaxation Response__* (p. 92), *__Relaxation Response Instructions__* (p. 95), *__Focus Word or Phrase__* (p. 96), *__Common Focus Word or Phrases__* (p. 97), and *__"Mini" Relaxation Exercises__* (p. 98) all describe the technique well. Often, I continue to use mantra meditation in my daily life. It helps to keep me in the present moment.

I do want to add a note of caution about selecting your mantra. Powerful mantras are often individualized, often have special meaning to the user. But they should be **spiritually uplifting**.

Most people would say that should be obvious, but experience teaches me otherwise. I once had a student who chose the following mantra: "Hate" on the in-breath, and "Kill" on the out-breath. Unfortunately, he practiced this mantra for several weeks before I learned what he was doing.

The Method of Christian Centering Prayer (p. 123) is another possibility. Proponents insist it is not mantra meditation, but in many ways it certainly looks like it. One difference cited is that a mantra is loudly repeated, totally occupying the mind, while the sacred word is introduced gently, "as laying a feather on a piece of absorbent cotton." [Keating, T. (1995). *The method of centering prayer*. Butler, NJ: Contemplative Outreach. Used with permission.] I am not going to argue such distinctions, because I have great respect for both traditions.

And I urge you not to disregard Centering Prayer because you are not a Christian. Please always keep in mind, "Truth is One; Paths are many." If you read Father Thomas Keating's writings, it is obvious he has spent many hours in God-consciousness. Many points in Centering Prayer apply to all meditation techniques and are worth your time studying.

Over the years, I have had several opportunities to go to a state prison and talk to inmates about stress management and meditation/prayer. **_The Method of Christian Centering Prayer_** (p. 123) would be one of my handouts. Almost every time I spoke to a group, at the end of the presentation, some inmates would return handouts on Christian Centering Prayer – so strong were their emotions about Christianity that they obviously felt they could learn nothing useful.

Other meditation techniques that I have found useful are listening to the inner sound or contemplating the inner light. As you have read, this book documents how, over years of practice, I internally became quiet enough to hear the inner sound of Om (Aum) within me. It is now with me, comforting me, always. Sometimes, though, I still have to make an intentional effort to quiet myself before I can actually hear it.

I have only experienced the inner light a few times. When it has appeared, it has filled me with such rapture!!! I know several people who report easily seeing the inner light and I envy them this ability. The **_Technique of Primordial Sound and Light Contemplation_** (p. 87) describes how you can develop the ability to hear the inner sound and/or see the inner light, if you desire.

When you see the inner light or hear the inner sound, follow it to its source, to Self- and God-realization.

Uninterrupted Awareness

For most folks, to achieve "uninterrupted awareness" requires a great deal of practice. The mind is like a wild, drunken monkey trapped in a cage. To tame it requires a lot of loving patience. I have now been meditating for almost thirty years, and there still are days that I experience "monkey mind." When I remind myself that God loves me just as I am, I am encouraged and continue my practice.

To be successful in meditation/prayer usually requires consistent effort, determination, and practice over a long period of time. It also requires you to develop a strong moral foundation. **_Yoga Philosophy_** (p. 105), **_Integral Yoga_**® (p. 107), and **_Raja Yoga: The Yoga of Meditation_** (p. 108) expound this truth.

Until you live a virtuous life, success in meditation/prayer is doubtful. How does one who covets, lies, cheats, steals, kills, and engages in sexual misconduct quiet the mind? That mind will always be agitated!

If you do not develop a strong moral foundation, you may learn powerful meditation techniques, but your life and consciousness will not be transformed. You will never harvest the fruits of the spirit – a loving, compassionate heart filled with peace and joy.

Remember, meditation/prayer is not about getting high; it is not about bliss. Often, I have to remind myself not to be too satisfied resting in Bliss-consciousness. As much as I love it, that is not my goal.

Rather, my goal is Self- and God-realization. I once asked Roy Eugene Davis, my guru (teacher), how I could become fully Self- and God-realized. He laughed and said that he wished he could tell me but he could not. Then he gently explained that is a path I have to discover for myself.

You, too, will have to discover the path for yourself. I wish you God speed on this very special journey and stand ready to assist you in any way that I can.

My Current Practice

Now that I am retired from my college, Panther Brook Spiritual Center is my ministry, my opportunity to be of service to others. There I teach what I have found to be useful in my own spiritual growth. There I lead souls to God! (So I did, after some delay, grow up to be a minister.)

The renewal of the spiritual life is facilitated by meditation/prayer, silence, solitude, and a natural environment. I have a firm belief that what I am offering at Panther Brook Spiritual Center is badly needed by the world – a beautiful, quiet setting for private retreats, both individual and small groups; a place to reconnect to one's true self; a place to rediscover the peace and joy within. And, from one's True Self, go into the world and serve others with more joy, compassion, and peace.

As I maintain my meditation practice on a regular basis, it continues to flourish! I often get wonderfully high, filled with bliss, and very relaxed. Still, I sometimes lose my ability to be a "silent witness" to events, lose my balance. But I feel that losing my balance occurs less frequently now.

I am becoming steadier, more solid. I note that, when I become anxious about something, I am better able to let it go. I seem to be gradually increasing my ability to rest in superconsciousness, my ability to permanently reside in God Consciousness.

Though the Serenity Meditation was my "hook" into meditation practice, I rarely use it now. As with all meditation/prayer techniques, once the mind is settled and focused, they are no longer necessary.

It was actually very difficult to let go of the Serenity Meditation, as I was quite attached to it. After years of practice, I began to flow easily into superconscious meditative states. At times I could even maintain relaxed, focused, uninterrupted awareness. Then I would remember, "Oh, I forgot to do the Serenity Meditation."

I would then go back and do it, even though it was totally unnecessary. I had already reached the point where the Serenity Meditation would take me. Eventually, I understood that it was time to let go of the meditation technique. It had served its purpose.

When my mind does need help settling down and focusing, I do Kriya Pranayama, or mantra. I often use a mantra recommended by Swami Satchidananda, "Om, Shanti," which translates as "God, Peace." As I breathe in, I mentally chant "Om," and, as I breathe out, I mentally chant "Shanti." As I mentally chant, I consciously make my out breath longer than my in breath.

Through my meditation/prayer practices, I have experienced the truth of Christ's words, "The Kingdom of God is within you" (Luke 17:21, KJV). Millions of people consider the beginning of their meditation/prayer practice their "spiritual birthday" – a date critical to their spiritual growth. Certainly that is true for me.

As I learned more about yoga and began to practice its teachings, I learned to listen to the inner sound, the sound of Om, of God, who is always with me, surrounding me, comforting me. I discovered that, at the deepest level of my being, I am joyously peaceful. Besides the increased joy and peace meditation/prayer brought into my life, I also experienced the other fruits of spiritual growth which are energizing and vitalizing, including a more loving and compassionate heart.

I know that the purpose of my life is to be Self- and God-realized, loving and serving God. My meditation/prayer practice and being of service to others are the most effective ways to fulfill that purpose.

If there has been one theme in my life, it has been a deep and constant desire for a reunion with God, a desire to serve God, and a desire to enter into the Kingdom of God. Through God's grace, I have, at times, fulfilled this desire.

Made in the USA
Monee, IL
20 November 2022

18209745R00105